WILLIAMS-SONOMA

Holiday Cooking with Kids

Recipes for Kids Ages 9 to 13

GENERAL EDITOR
Chuck Williams

RECIPES
Susan Manlin Katzman

PHOTOGRAPHY
Joyce Oudkerk Pool

TIME
LIFE
BOOKS

TIME-LIFE BOOKS
Time-Life Books is a division of Time Life Inc.
Time-Life is a trademark of Time Warner Inc. U.S.A.

TIME-LIFE CUSTOM PUBLISHING
Vice President and Publisher: Terry Newell
Vice President of Sales and Marketing: Neil Levin
Director of Financial Operations: J. Brian Birky
Director of Acquisitions: Jennifer L. Pearce

WILLIAMS-SONOMA
Founder and Vice-Chairman: Chuck Williams
Associate Book Buyer: Cecilia Michaelis

WELDON OWEN INC.
President: John Owen
Vice President and Publisher: Wendely Harvey
Chief Operating Officer: Larry Partington
Vice President International Sales: Stuart Laurence
Managing Editor: Val Cipollone
Consulting Editor: Norman Kolpas
Copy Editor: Sharon Silva
Series Design: Kari Perin, Perin+Perin
Book Design: Diane Dempsey
Production Director: Stephanie Sherman
Production Manager: Christine DePedro
Production Editor: Sarah Lemas
Food Stylist: Andrea Lucich
Prop Stylist: Rebecca Stephany
Studio Assistant: Arjen Kammeraad
Food Styling Assistant: Elisabet der Nederlanden
Glossary Illustrations: Alice Harth

The Williams-Sonoma Lifestyles Series
conceived and produced by Weldon Owen Inc.
814 Montgomery Street, San Francisco, CA 94133

In collaboration with Williams-Sonoma
3250 Van Ness Avenue, San Francisco, CA 94109

Separations by Colourscan Overseas Co. Pte. Ltd.
Printed in Singapore by Tien Wah Press (Pte.) Ltd.

A WELDON OWEN PRODUCTION
Copyright © 1999 Weldon Owen Inc.
All rights reserved, including the right of repro-
duction in whole or in part in any form.

First printed in 1999
10 9 8 7 6 5 4 3 2 1

Library of Congress
Cataloging-in-Publication Data

Katzman, Susan Manlin.
    Holiday cooking with kids / general editor, Chuck
Williams; recipes, Susan Manlin Katzman;
photography, Joyce Oudkerk Pool.
        p.   cm. — (Williams-Sonoma lifestyles)
    Includes index.
    ISBN 0-7370-2025-3
    I. Holiday cookery. II. Cookery — Juvenile
literature. I. Williams, Chuck.   II. Title.
III. Series.
TX739.K28 1999
641.5'68—dc21   99-10023
                                              CIP

A NOTE ON SAFETY
The publisher and the author have made every effort
to emphasize the importance of safety procedures
when children are cooking in the kitchen. Neither the
publisher nor the author can assume responsibility
for any accident, injuries, losses, or other damages
resulting from the use of this book. Children should
not use this cookbook without adult supervision.

A NOTE ON NUTRITIONAL ANALYSIS
Each recipe is analyzed for significant nutrients per
serving. Not included in the analysis are ingredients
that are optional or added to taste, or are suggested
as an alternative or substitution either in the recipe
or in the recipe introduction or accompanying tip.
In recipes that yield a range of servings, the analysis
is for the middle of that range.

Contents

8 SPRING HOLIDAYS   10 SUMMER HOLIDAYS

12 AUTUMN HOLIDAYS   14 WINTER HOLIDAYS

16 BASIC RECIPES   19 TIPS FOR KIDS IN THE HOLIDAY KITCHEN

20 Spring Holiday Recipes

48 Summer Holiday Recipes

62 Autumn Holiday Recipes

80 Winter Holiday Recipes

108 GLOSSARY   112 INDEX

Welcome

Some of my happiest childhood memories are of the times I spent helping my grandmother cook for the holidays. We went all out at Thanksgiving and Christmas, and she gave me lots of jobs to do, from basting the turkey to making gravy to baking cookies. I enjoyed working with her and felt justifiably proud of the compliments our cooking received. That pride, which all children feel when they contribute something to a family occasion, is the reason behind this book, the goal of which is to involve children in the preparation of holiday meals.

To accomplish that goal in a way that works enjoyably and efficiently for grown-ups and children alike, the book is organized by seasons and by individual holidays. On the following pages, the 11 holidays covered are introduced with a bit of history and folklore that adults and kids can share. These season-by-season pages are followed on page 19 by important safety tips everyone should review beforehand.

The 44 recipes that make up most of the book have been created and written to be easy enough for a child aged 9 to 13 to follow, although adult supervision is still a good idea. All of them produce wonderful holiday foods that both grown-ups and kids will enjoy.

Happy holidays and happy cooking!

Chuck Williams

Spring Holidays

Mother's Day is celebrated on the second Sunday of May. Use a tray (above) to serve your mom breakfast in bed.

All kinds of holidays happen in spring, and there's lots of great food to go along with them. From Valentine's Day to Mother's Day, you'll have loads of fun cooking and baking this time of year.

Valentine's Day

When Valentine's Day arrives on February 14, spring is still officially over a month away. But with its heart-shaped treats and bright red flowers, this day for sharing thoughts of love reminds us that sunnier days are just around the corner.

Americans have been exchanging valentines since 1902. Some of the best valentine presents are sweet foods that are shaped into hearts to symbolize love. Candies are always a favorite, and so are cookies decorated to look like big versions of the little candy "conversation hearts." With a bit of imagination, you can give someone special a valentine any time of day. Have you ever made a breakfast valentine? Turn to page 21 and you'll see how.

Easter

Easter comes at the time of year when all kinds of people all around the world have long celebrated the arrival of spring. That's why the things we see a lot of in spring—eggs, chicks, bunnies, and flowers—are the same things we see at Easter.

Decorating eggs is especially fun, but have you ever thought of decorating eggs with onion skins? You'll find an unusual trick for coloring eggs with natural dyes on page 32. They'll look great in Easter baskets!

Eggs are just a start at Easter. Many families enjoy preparing a special festive menu for Easter supper, and there's plenty of

opportunity for kids to help out. If you like to bake, try making the delicious little strawberry tartlets on page 41.

Passover

Passover is a Jewish holiday that lasts eight days. On the first or second night of Passover, families traditionally prepare a celebratory dinner called a Seder. Many of the foods served that night have symbolic meanings and are presented on a special Seder plate. Matzo Ball Soup (page 27) and matzo, an unleavened bread, are often served, and matzo meal is used in place of flour. Did you know you can make brownies from matzo meal? Turn to page 31 and you'll see how. Like Easter, Passover is celebrated in spring, a time of birth and renewal.

Mother's Day

In 1914, President Woodrow Wilson proclaimed Mother's Day an official American celebration, held each year on the second Sunday of May.

The point of Mother's Day is to let Mom know how much you appreciate her. One great way to show you care is to serve her breakfast in bed. Set up a tray with a homemade feast and some pretty flowers (opposite page). For the perfect menu, make a soft-boiled egg, scones, and a colorful fruit salad.

The Seder plate (left) is a traditional part of Passover. Each section of the plate holds a different type of food. Haroset (page 28), an apple-and-nut condiment, is a good recipe for kids to make and one that's included in the Seder plate.

PREPARING STRAWBERRIES & ASPARAGUS

When preparing strawberries for a springtime recipe, use a small sharp knife to cut off the green hulls. When serving berries whole, you can leave the hulls attached to use as handles, if you like.

Before cooking asparagus, you need to remove their tough stem ends. Grasp a spear with both hands and bend near the cut end. The asparagus will break at the point it first becomes tender.

Summer Holidays

Summertime is when we celebrate Father's Day. Pack a picnic for Dad (right) and take him out to the park or his favorite fishing hole. It's easy and fun to make decorations (above) for the Fourth of July. Hide little toys inside cardboard tubes and roll them up in red, white, and blue tissue paper to make your own Fourth of July "firecrackers."

With school out, every summer day feels like a holiday. It's the perfect time of year for families to have backyard barbecues and picnics in the park. Kids can help.

Father's Day

Can you guess which holiday was the inspiration for Father's Day? That's right: Mother's Day. A woman named Sonora Smart Dodd organized the first Father's Day celebration in Spokane, Washington, on her own dad's birthday. The celebration caught on, but it took many years for Father's Day to be officially recognized. Finally, in 1964, President Lyndon Johnson proclaimed the third Sunday of every June a special day for dads.

One of the best ways kids can celebrate Father's Day is to think of the kinds of foods their dads love to eat and then plan a special menu. A picnic lunch with a great, big Hero Sandwich (page 53) might be high on the list. Make a bowl of Favorite Potato Salad (page 50), too. And, if it's hot outside, Dad might like to cool down with a Frozen Fruit Pop. Turn to page 49 and you'll find a dessert treat guaranteed to chase away summer's heat.

Independence Day

Summertime's big-bang holiday is the Fourth of July. It's a day-long celebration, marking our country's declaration of independence from Great Britain. There are local parades in the morning, games and barbecues in the afternoon, and bright, noisy displays of fireworks all evening long.

Of course, from morning until night there's all kinds of great food to make. It's especially fun to find summertime ingredients that come in patriotic colors: look for ruby red berries and bright red tomatoes, white (or pale yellow) sweet corn and bananas, and sapphire blue blueberries and blue corn chips. Pick your favorites and have a happy Fourth!

SUMMERTIME CONFETTI PUNCH

INGREDIENTS
1½ cups orange juice
1 can (46 ounces) unsweetened pineapple juice
1 bottle (32 ounces) cranberry-apple drink
1 bottle (24 ounces) grape juice
¼ cup granulated sugar
¼ cup water
⅓ cup lemon juice
1 bottle (32 ounces) sparkling water

EQUIPMENT
measuring cups
can opener
3 plastic ice-cube trays
small saucepan
long-handled wooden spoon
hot pad
pot holders
large punch bowl with cups
ladle

SERVES 12

1. Fill the ice-cube trays with the orange juice, pineapple juice, cranberry-apple drink, and grape juice. Do not mix the juices in the compartments, and make an equal number of cubes of each different drink. Refrigerate the remaining pineapple, cranberry-apple, and grape juices. Put the ice-cube trays in your freezer until the juice cubes are frozen solid. (Complete this step the night before you serve this punch, so the cubes have plenty of time to freeze.)

2. Put the sugar and water in the saucepan. Set the pan on a burner of your stove and turn on the heat to medium. Cook the mixture, stirring constantly with the wooden spoon, until the sugar dissolves, about 1 minute. Continue cooking without stirring until the mixture comes to a boil. Boil for 1 minute. Turn off the heat. Put the hot pad on your counter. Using pot holders, transfer the saucepan to the hot pad and let the mixture cool completely.

3. Put the lemon juice in the punch bowl. Add the cooled sugar-water mixture and the remaining pineapple, cranberry-apple, and grape juices. Uncap the sparkling water and add it to the punch bowl. Stir the mixture. Add the frozen juice cubes to the punch.

4. Ladle the punch into cups. Make sure each serving gets different-colored juice cubes. Serve immediately.

Autumn Holidays

Carving pumpkins is an autumn tradition for adults and kids to share.

When green leaves turn brilliant shades of gold, red, orange, and yellow, food stores and farmers' markets fill up with a rich harvest of fruits and vegetables. Autumn is a season of wonderful holidays and of lots of wonderful food kids can make.

Halloween

October 31 is the spookiest day of the year. Halloween has long been a holiday for tricks and treats, but the treats are by far the sweetest today. The Halloween tradition of trick-or-treating began long ago in Great Britain with children collecting little gifts of sweet rolls, money, or fresh-picked autumn fruits. It was not until the 19th century that candy became the preferred American treat, and it remains the favorite of kids today.

Pumpkins, too, are a popular part of Halloween, especially when they're carved into funny or scary jack-o'-lanterns. You should ask an adult for help with the carving and with lighting the candle inside, but you can draw the face on the pumpkin and watch as your creation is carefully cut out.

Halloween was made for kids, and kids can help make the day even more fun. Plan a party and invite your friends to join you for a ghoulish feast. Turn to page 66 for rich, chocolaty cupcakes known as devil's food. There are cookies to bake and decorate for the season and apples to dip in rich, gooey caramel. You'll also find a wickedly spiced cider recipe that can be served warm or cold—the best witches' brew!

Thanksgiving

In October 1621, a year after their arrival in Plymouth, Massachusetts, the pilgrims held a three-day Thanksgiving festival to celebrate their first successful harvest in the New World. With the help of Native Americans, they had learned to raise crops, pick wild plants, tap maple syrup, and gather other local foods. To give thanks for their good fortune, they prepared a feast that included corn and squashes they had grown, along with fish and meats. Nobody knows for sure, however, if turkey was served at the first Thanksgiving, but wild turkeys lived in the woodlands nearby.

Today that first feast is celebrated each year on the fourth Thursday in November, with a turkey often served as the main course. And while the grown-ups are busy roasting the bird, kids can join in the fun of preparing the family meal by making some of the traditional side dishes featuring autumn ingredients, such as sweet-tart cranberries and sweet, creamy acorn squash. Of course, Thanksgiving also gives us a bounty of leftovers, ready to turn into great sandwiches the next day.

At Thanksgiving, kids can help decorate as well as cook. Make a beautiful centerpiece (above, left) for the dinner table with small pumpkins, gourds, and autumn leaves. An adult should help with lighting the candles.

CORING APPLES

Before including an apple in some salads or cooked dishes, you may need to cut out its tough core and seeds. Steady the fruit, stem end up, on a cutting board. With a sharp knife, cut it in half straight down through the stem end. Cut each half in half again. Then, with a small, sharp knife, carefully cut out the core section from each quarter.

Winter Holidays

Holiday Cookies and Carolers' Hot Chocolate are wonderful wintertime treats (top). Dreidels (above) spin for Hanukkah.

In winter, when the days are cold and dark, we celebrate three of the year's brightest and warmest holidays. Best of all, Hanukkah, Christmas, and New Year's present all kinds of opportunities for kids to cook and bake.

Hanukkah

Hanukkah is the Jewish Festival of Lights. At sundown for eight nights, families light candles— one on the first night, two on the second, and so on—to celebrate the rededication of the Temple of Jerusalem more than two thousand years ago. They sing songs, exchange gifts, and play a game of chance called dreidel by spinning a special four-sided top of the same name.

Hanukkah dinner is a celebration, too. Kids can help prepare big and small parts of the meal. A whole roast chicken is sometimes served. Turn to page 80 and find out just how simple a recipe it is. You might also choose to make the Potato Latkes on page 83, a Hanukkah tradition, or a special sparkling dessert called Golden Gelt (page 84).

Christmas

Food plays a big role during the Christmas holiday, a time when colorful decorations, traditional songs, gift giving, and parties are all part of the season's festivities. A lot of time and thought goes into preparing the big Christmas dinner, but you can also make all kinds of wonderful foods to give as gifts. It's fun to turn foods into decorations, too, such as stringing cranberries and popcorn for hanging on the Christmas tree.

Baking Christmas cookies is a favorite tradition, and kids can go to town when it comes to icing and decorating. Of course,

Christmas cookies are great to eat, but they can also be festively wrapped and given as special homemade gifts.

Many festive meals can be served, from a tree-trimming party with Carolers' Hot Chocolate (page 103) and Holiday Cookies (page 100), both fun recipes for kids to make, to a cozy family breakfast, to a glorious dinner on Christmas Day. The dinner is one of the most elaborate menus families serve all year long, which means that kids get the chance to make all kinds of special recipes, from airy Popovers (page 96) to a spicy-sweet Old-Fashioned Gingerbread (page 99) that no one will be able to resist.

New Year's

Kids can have a great time ringing in the new year with party hats and noisemakers. But no matter what sort of celebration your family traditionally plans for this festive time, you can be a part of making it special.

Whether it's ordering your favorite takeout, eating big bowls of soup by the fire, or making breakfast together on New Year's Day, there are many ways that kids can help. If a special treat for New Year's Eve is desired, try making Chocolate Fondue (page 107) or the kid-friendly New Year's Toasts on page 104. Both are great ways to wish friends and family a very happy new year!

PEELING PEARS

When a recipe directs you to peel a pear, use a vegetable peeler to get the job done. Hold the pear in one hand or steady it against a cutting board. Starting at the stem end, peel the skin from the pear in long, even strips with the vegetable peeler. Turn the pear and peel away another strip. Continue turning and peeling until all the skin is removed.

To transfer the dough to the pie dish, roll it around the rolling pin. Hold the rolling pin over the dish and carefully unwrap the dough, letting it fall gently into the dish. With your fingers, ease the dough into the bottom and up the side of the dish.

There should be about 1 inch of dough hanging over the side of the pie dish. To crimp the edge of the dough, pinch it between your fingers, using your thumb as a guide. Work your way all the way around the edge.

Basic Pie Pastry

MAKES ENOUGH PASTRY FOR
SIX 5-INCH TARTLETS OR
ONE 9-INCH PIE SHELL

INGREDIENTS

1 cup all-purpose flour
2 tablespoons sugar (optional)
½ teaspoon salt
7 tablespoons solid vegetable
  shortening
3 tablespoons ice water
flour for kneading and rolling dough

EQUIPMENT

measuring cups and spoons
medium mixing bowl
large spoon
pastry blender
table fork
plastic wrap
rolling pin

1. Put the flour, sugar (if using), and salt in the mixing bowl. Stir with the large spoon to mix. Put each tablespoon of the shortening in a different place on top of the flour. With your fingertips or the pastry blender, very lightly and quickly mix the shortening with the flour mixture to form crumbs about the size of peas. (Always mix the pastry dough lightly and quickly; dough that is handled too much will make a tough crust.)

2. Sprinkle the ice water, 1 tablespoon at a time, over the top of the flour mixture. Stir the mixture with the fork until it is moist and holds together.

3. Lightly sprinkle a flat work surface with flour. Turn the dough out of the bowl onto the floured surface. With your fingertips, lightly and quickly knead the dough just until it is smooth, about 15 strokes.

4. Gather the dough together with your hands and form it into a ball. Flatten the ball into a thick circle. Wrap the circle in plastic wrap and refrigerate until chilled, at least 20 minutes or up to 1 hour.

5. To roll out the dough, sprinkle a flat work surface lightly with flour. Sprinkle the rolling pin with flour. Remove the dough from the refrigerator, unwrap it, and place it on the floured work surface. Flatten the dough lightly with your rolling pin. Roll out the dough with the rolling pin from the center to the edge with light, even strokes. Occasionally lift and rotate the dough so that it doesn't stick to the work surface. The shape should be about 1 inch larger on all sides than the pan you are using and it should be ⅛ to ¼ inch thick.

6. Cut out, shape, and bake the pastry dough according to the recipes for Strawberry Tartlets on page 41 or for Favorite Pumpkin Pie on page 77.

ROLLING & CUTTING

To roll out the cookie dough, apply firm, even pressure with the rolling pin. Roll the dough from the center to the edges.

To cut out shapes, hold the cookie cutter firmly and press straight down through the dough. Lift the cookie cutter and press it down to cut out another shape. Keep the shapes as close together as possible and cut out as many as you can.

PREP TIP: Making and working with dough can be tricky. You may need to ask an adult for help.

Basic Butter Cookie Dough

MAKES ENOUGH DOUGH FOR
ABOUT 40 COOKIES

INGREDIENTS

1½ cups all-purpose flour
1 teaspoon baking powder
¼ teaspoon salt
½ cup unsalted butter, softened
¾ cup granulated sugar
1 egg
1½ teaspoons vanilla extract
flour for rolling dough

EQUIPMENT

measuring cups and spoons
medium mixing bowl
wooden spoon
large mixing bowl
electric mixer
plastic wrap
rolling pin

1. Put the flour, baking powder, and salt in the medium mixing bowl. Stir with the wooden spoon until the ingredients are mixed. Set the bowl aside.

2. Put the butter and sugar in the large mixing bowl. With the electric mixer set on medium-high speed, beat until the mixture is well combined. Add the egg and vanilla and beat until light and creamy. With the mixer on low speed, gradually beat in the flour mixture until blended.

3. Gather the dough together into one mass and divide the dough in half. Shape each half into a ball. Pat the top of each ball to flatten it into a thick circle. Wrap each dough circle in plastic wrap and place it in the refrigerator until it is firm enough to roll out, about 1 hour.

4. To roll out the dough, lightly sprinkle flour over a flat work surface. Sprinkle the rolling pin with flour. Remove 1 piece of the dough from the refrigerator. Unwrap the dough and place it on the floured work surface. With the rolling pin, roll out the dough into a large circle about ⅛ inch thick. Occasionally lift and rotate the dough so that it doesn't stick to the work surface.

5. Cut out, shape, and bake the cookie dough according to the recipes for Be Mine Cookies on page 22 or Holiday Cookies on page 100.

COOKING TIP: To make chocolate icing, add ¼ cup unsweetened cocoa powder to the confectioners' sugar before sifting.

Basic Icing

MAKES ABOUT ¾ CUP

INGREDIENTS	EQUIPMENT
2 tablespoons unsalted butter	measuring cups and spoons
2 cups confectioners' sugar, or as needed	small saucepan
	sifter
1 teaspoon vanilla extract	medium mixing bowl
2 tablespoons heavy cream or milk, or as needed	electric mixer

1. Put the butter in the small saucepan. Set the saucepan on a burner of your stove and turn the heat on to low. Heat only until the butter melts. Then turn off the heat.

2. Put the 2 cups confectioners' sugar into the sifter and sift into the medium mixing bowl. Add the melted butter, vanilla, and 2 tablespoons cream or milk. With the electric mixer set on medium speed, beat the mixture until smooth and creamy. If necessary, add more cream or milk to make the icing spreadable, or more sugar to make the icing stiffer. Use the icing immediately.

Sweetened Whipped Cream

MAKES 2 CUPS

INGREDIENTS	EQUIPMENT
1 cup heavy cream, chilled	measuring cups and spoons
2 to 3 teaspoons sugar	mixing bowl
¾ teaspoon vanilla extract	electric mixer

Pour the chilled cream into the mixing bowl. Add the sugar and the vanilla extract. With the electric mixer set on high speed, beat the cream until it thickens enough to form soft peaks. Do not overbeat or the cream will turn into butter.

WHIPPING CREAM

Whip cream just until soft peaks form. To check for soft peaks, turn the mixer off and pull the beaters out of the bowl. If the cream forms peaks that droop a little on the end of the beaters and in the bowl, it is done.

TIPS FOR KIDS IN THE HOLIDAY KITCHEN

Holiday cooking is a lot of fun. But with all the extra activity going on in and around the kitchen, you've got to be extra careful to put safety first. Read these tips before you start cooking. If you have questions about the way a recipe or piece of equipment is meant to work, ask an adult for help. When two people cook together, helping each other as they go, it's twice as much fun.

Before You Start Cooking

✔ Get an adult's permission. Cook only when an adult is home and able to help if necessary.

✔ Read the recipe you plan to make from start to finish. That way, you will know what to expect.

✔ Make sure you know how to use the equipment and appliances you'll need to cook and bake. If you have questions, ask an adult for help.

✔ Roll up your sleeves and tie back long hair. Put on an apron to keep your clothes clean. Wash your hands with warm water and soap before handling food.

✔ Assemble all the ingredients you will need for the recipe. Measure the ingredients as the recipe directs and have them all ready to go.

✔ Assemble all the equipment you will need for the recipe.

While You're Cooking

✔ Work as neatly as you can. As soon as something drops or spills, wipe up the mess.

✔ Keep pot holders, towels, and cookbooks well away from the oven and the stove top.

✔ Use only dry pot holders to pick up hot pans and plates. If you pick up something hot with a wet pot holder, you'll get a nasty burn. Heat travels quickly through water and dampness.

✔ Before removing a pan or dish from the oven, clear a space for it on the stove top. Or place a rack or hot pad on your counter for the hot pan.

✔ Lift lids from hot pots at an angle, away from you. This will let the hot steam from inside the pot rise up without coming toward you.

✔ Keep pan handles away from the edge of the stove and away from hot burners. That way, no one can knock them over or get burned.

✔ Make sure your hands are dry before you switch an electric appliance on or off. Never have wet hands when touching anything electrical.

✔ Turn off the motor of a blender or mixer before removing the lid or reaching into the work bowl.

✔ Stay in the kitchen while you are cooking. That way you can keep a close eye on the action.

✔ When it comes time for cleanup, remember that grease and water do not mix. If you have a hot pan with hot grease in it, let it cool safely out of the way before putting water in it. Water causes hot grease to splash and splatter.

✔ Always wash your hands with warm water and soap after handling food.

Knives and Other Sharp Tools

✔ When slicing or chopping, always place ingredients on a cutting board. Keep a good grip on the knife's handle and cut with the blade pointing away from you and with your fingers well clear of it.

✔ Always move cautiously and slowly when holding sharp tools.

✔ Wash knives and sharp tools individually. Never put them in a sinkful of soapy water. You might forget they are there and grab one by the blade. Keep knives and sharp tools safely stored when not in use.

In Case of Fire

You probably won't have to deal with a fire in the kitchen, but just in case one happens, call for help immediately. Don't try to handle a fire alone.

✔ Every kitchen should have a fire extinguisher. Know where yours is stored and how to use it.

Heart-Shaped Waffles

COOKING TIME: 20 MINUTES

INGREDIENTS

1 egg

1 cup milk

1 tablespoon vegetable oil for the batter

1 cup all-purpose flour

1 tablespoon granulated sugar

2 teaspoons baking powder

¼ teaspoon salt

vegetable oil for greasing waffle iron, if needed

¼ cup unsalted butter

¼ cup maple syrup or 4 tablespoons strawberry jam

2 cups sliced strawberries (optional)

EQUIPMENT

measuring cups and spoons

waffle iron

medium mixing bowl

small mixing bowl

table fork

electric mixer

rubber spatula

pastry brush, if needed

ladle

serving plate

Heart-shaped waffles are a special Valentine's Day treat. The number of waffles the recipe yields will vary according to the size of your waffle iron. If you don't have a heart-shaped waffle iron, use this same recipe to make square, round, or rectangular waffles.

SERVES 4

1. Read the instructions that came with your waffle iron. Preheat the waffle iron as directed.

2. Separate the egg, putting the yolk in the medium bowl and the white in the small mixing bowl. Set the white aside.

3. Add the milk and the 1 tablespoon oil to the yolk. With the fork, beat the mixture until it is blended. Add the flour, sugar, baking powder, and salt. Beat with the fork until the batter is smooth.

4. With the electric mixer set on high speed, beat the egg white until it stands in stiff peaks when you lift the beaters (turn the mixer off before lifting). With the spatula, carefully fold the egg white into the yolk mixture.

5. Not all waffle irons need to be greased (check the instructions). If yours does or if you want to be extra sure that your waffles don't stick, use the pastry brush to brush a light coating of vegetable oil over both grids of your iron.

6. Use the ladle to pour the batter into the center of the hot waffle iron until it is one-half to two-thirds covered. Close the iron. You will see steam rising from the sides. Cook until the steaming stops and the waffle is ready, about 4 minutes. To see if the waffle is cooked, lift the lid and peek. The lid should lift easily and the waffle should be golden brown. If the lid doesn't lift easily or the color is too light, close the iron and bake the waffle a little longer.

7. With the fork, carefully loosen the waffle and transfer it to the serving plate. Repeat with the remaining batter. Serve the waffles hot with the butter, syrup or jam, and with the sliced strawberries, if you like.

NUTRITIONAL ANALYSIS PER SERVING: Calories 389 (Kilojoules 1,634); Protein 7 g; Carbohydrates 49 g; Total Fat 19 g; Saturated Fat 9 g; Cholesterol 93 mg; Sodium 438 mg; Dietary Fiber 3 g

Be Mine Cookies

COOKING TIME: 12 MINUTES

INGREDIENTS

1 recipe Basic Butter Cookie Dough
(page 17)

solid vegetable shortening for
greasing baking sheets

2 recipes Basic Icing (page 18)

red and blue food coloring

EQUIPMENT

2 baking sheets

heart-shaped cookie cutters

metal spatula

rolling pin

cooling racks

hot pads

pot holders

rubber spatula

3 small bowls

2 mixing spoons

table knife

pastry bag with plain writing tip

COOKING TIP: You can make as many
different colors of icing as you like.
When decorating, use one color on
the bottom and another color on top.

Baking these heart-shaped cookies is a wonderful way to say "I
love you."

MAKES ABOUT 40 COOKIES

1. Prepare the cookie dough and roll out as directed. Adjust 2 oven racks
to be in the center of your oven. Turn the oven on to 350°F. Lightly
grease the baking sheets with the vegetable shortening.

2. Using a heart-shaped cookie cutter, press it straight down into the
dough to cut out a shape, then lift carefully. Repeat, cutting close to the
first one, until you have cut out as many cookies as you can. Gently slip
the metal spatula under the dough shapes and transfer to the baking
sheets. Set the scraps aside. Roll out and cut the second piece of dough.
Transfer to the baking sheets. Gather all the dough scraps together,
then roll out, cut, and transfer to the baking sheets.

3. Place the baking sheets on the center racks in the preheated oven.
Bake until the cookies are light golden brown around the edges, 10 to 12
minutes.

4. Put the cooling racks and hot pads on your counter. With pot holders,
transfer the baking sheets to the hot pads. With the metal spatula, transfer the cookies to the racks. Let cool completely.

5. Prepare the Basic Icing. With the rubber spatula, divide the icing
evenly between the 3 small bowls; set 1 bowl aside. Tint 1 bowl of icing
a very pale pink by adding 1 or 2 drops of red food coloring. Tint the
remaining bowl of icing a shade of purple. (To make purple, mix 1 or 2
drops of red coloring with 1 or 2 drops of blue.) You should have 1 bowl
each of white, pink, and purple icing.

6. With the knife, spread a thin layer of icing over each cookie.

7. With the rubber spatula, put some icing in the pastry bag fitted with the
writing tip and decorate the hearts. Let dry completely, about 30 minutes.
Store in an airtight container at room temperature for up to 3 days.

NUTRITIONAL ANALYSIS PER COOKIE: Calories 120 (Kilojoules 504); Protein 1 g;
Carbohydrates 20 g; Total Fat 4 g; Saturated Fat 3 g; Cholesterol 17 mg; Sodium 29 mg;
Dietary Fiber 0 g

Valentine Mints

INGREDIENTS

about 2½ cups confectioners' sugar

2 tablespoons unsalted butter,
    at room temperature

about 1½ tablespoons warm water

½ teaspoon peppermint extract, plus
    extra as needed

red food coloring

confectioners' sugar for rolling mints

EQUIPMENT

measuring cups and spoons

fine-mesh sieve

table spoon

2 medium mixing bowls

electric mixer

waxed paper

rolling pin

1-inch heart-shaped cutter

baking sheet

PREP TIP: If you have a sifter you
use for sifting dry ingredients, use
the sifter instead of the sieve.

One of the sweetest ways to say Happy Valentine's Day is to
make your valentine a batch of old-fashioned butter mints.

MAKES ABOUT 50 MINTS

1. First, you need to sift the confectioners' sugar: Put it in the fine-mesh sieve, a little at a time, and press it through the sieve with the back of the spoon into a measuring cup. You will need 2¼ cups sifted sugar.

2. Put 1 cup of the sifted sugar, the butter, and 1 tablespoon of the warm water in a medium bowl. With the electric mixer set on medium speed, beat until the mixture is smooth and well blended. Slowly add the remaining 1½ cups sifted sugar and ½ tablespoon water, continuing to beat until the mixture is smooth and well blended. The sugar mixture should be soft and not sticky. If it is crumbly, add a few drops of water. If it is sticky, add a little confectioners' sugar.

3. Add the peppermint extract to the sugar mixture. With your hand, knead in the extract by squeezing and pressing it into the mixture. Taste and knead in a few more drops of peppermint extract if you want a stronger peppermint flavor.

4. Divide the mixture in half. Put one-half in a separate medium bowl and leave the other half in the first bowl. Add 1 or 2 drops of red food coloring to the mixture in one bowl and knead it in until the dough is evenly pink. Add 3 or 4 drops of red food coloring to the remaining mixture and knead until evenly red.

5. Lightly dust or rub 2 large sheets of waxed paper with confectioners' sugar. Place the pink sugar mixture on 1 sheet of waxed paper and cover it with the other. Make sure the sugar-rubbed side of the paper is against the sugar mixture. With the rolling pin, roll out the mixture ⅛ inch thick. Peel off the top sheet of paper. With the small heart-shaped cutter, cut out the mints. Repeat the rolling and cutting with the red mixture. Carefully transfer the cut-out mints to a baking sheet lined with a clean sheet of waxed paper. Set aside until firm, about 1 hour.

6. Store the mints in an airtight container in a cool place for up to 3 days.

NUTRITIONAL ANALYSIS PER MINT: Calories 30 (Kilojoules 126); Protein 0 g;
Carbohydrates 7 g; Total Fat 0 g; Saturated Fat 0 g; Cholesterol 1 mg; Sodium 5 mg;
Dietary Fiber 0 g

Matzo Ball Soup

COOKING TIME: 35 MINUTES

INGREDIENTS

2 eggs

3 tablespoons vegetable oil

1 tablespoon water

½ cup matzo meal

1 teaspoon salt

8 cups chicken broth

EQUIPMENT

measuring cups and spoons

small mixing bowl

table fork

aluminum foil or plastic wrap

3-quart soup pot with lid

slotted spoon

3-quart saucepan

ladle

6 soup bowls

SAFETY TIP: Ask an adult for help when it comes time to add the matzo balls to the pot of boiling water.

At Passover, an unleavened bread called matzo is served, and matzo meal is used in place of flour. The dumplings in this soup are made with matzo meal, and the soup is so delicious that it is eaten not only at Passover, but throughout the year.

SERVES 6

1. Put the eggs, oil, and water in the small bowl. Beat with the fork until well blended. Add the matzo meal and salt and stir until the ingredients are well combined. Cover the bowl with aluminum foil or plastic wrap and refrigerate until firm, about 30 minutes.

2. Pour enough water into the soup pot to fill it three-fourths full. Set the pot on your stove, turn the heat on to high, and bring the water to a rapid boil. (A rapid boil is when the bubbles are big, they rise to the surface quickly, and they break apart immediately.) Immediately reduce the heat so that the water boils very gently. (A gentle boil is when the bubbles are small, they rise slowly, and there are not too many of them.)

3. Wet your hands with cool water and form the matzo-meal mixture into 6 equal-sized balls. Being very careful to avoid splashes, using the slotted spoon, gently slip the balls into the gently boiling water. Cover the pot and cook the matzo balls at a gentle boil for 35 minutes.

4. Meanwhile, pour the broth into the saucepan. Set the pan on your stove, turn the heat on to medium, and bring the broth to a gentle boil. Reduce the heat to low so the broth simmers. (When the broth is at a simmer, only an occasional bubble rises to the surface.)

5. When the matzo balls are cooked, turn off the heat. Ladle the broth into the 6 soup bowls, dividing it evenly. With the slotted spoon, transfer 1 matzo ball to each soup bowl. Serve immediately.

NUTRITIONAL ANALYSIS PER SERVING: Calories 168 (Kilojoules 706); Protein 6 g; Carbohydrates 11 g; Total Fat 11 g; Saturated Fat 2 g; Cholesterol 71 mg; Sodium 1,743 mg; Dietary Fiber 0 g

Haroset

COOKING TIME: 15 MINUTES

INGREDIENTS

3 apples

¼ cup chopped walnuts or pecans

1 tablespoon granulated sugar

½ teaspoon ground cinnamon

2 tablespoons grape juice

EQUIPMENT

measuring cups and spoons

cutting board

small, sharp knife

medium mixing bowl

large spoon

serving bowl

plastic wrap

Haroset is served at a Passover Seder. It is a symbol of the mortar the Israelite slaves used to build the pyramids in Egypt and is one of the foods that is featured on the Seder plate. Many varieties of apples, the main ingredient in haroset, are available in supermarkets. While all apples can be eaten uncooked, some varieties taste better raw and some taste better cooked. Red Delicious and Granny Smith apples are particularly good for this dish.

MAKES ABOUT 2½ CUPS

1. Put an apple, stem end up, on the cutting board. With the sharp knife, cut the apple into quarters. Cut away the stem and the core from the apple quarters (throw the stem and core away). Cut the apple into small square pieces. Put the apple pieces in the medium bowl. Now quarter and chop the rest of the apples the same way and add them to the bowl.

2. Add the nuts, sugar, cinnamon, and grape juice to the apples. With the spoon, stir until the ingredients are well mixed. Transfer the mixture to a pretty serving bowl. Cover the bowl with plastic wrap and refrigerate until serving. Serve well chilled.

NUTRITIONAL ANALYSIS PER ¼-CUP SERVING: Calories 50 (Kilojoules 212); Protein 1 g; Carbohydrates 9 g; Total Fat 2 g; Saturated Fat 0 g; Cholesterol 0 mg; Sodium 0 mg; Dietary Fiber 1 g

Chocolate Chip Passover Brownies

COOKING TIME: 25 MINUTES

INGREDIENTS

vegetable oil for greasing pan

2 eggs

½ cup vegetable oil

1 cup granulated sugar

¼ teaspoon salt

¼ cup unsweetened cocoa powder

½ cup matzo cake meal

⅔ cup semisweet chocolate chips

confectioners' sugar for dusting
  (optional)

EQUIPMENT

measuring cups and spoons

pastry brush

8-inch square baking pan

large mixing bowl

electric mixer

rubber spatula

toothpick

cooling rack

pot holders

table knife

serving plate

So much food is served at a traditional Passover feast that most people are full before they reach dessert. But, it seems, there is always room for dessert. During Passover, these brownies must be made with matzo cake meal, which is matzo ground to a fine flour. At other times of the year, you can make these brownies with all-purpose flour, substituting ⅔ cup flour for the ½ cup cake meal.

MAKES 16 BROWNIES

1. Adjust an oven rack to be in the center of your oven without another rack above it. Turn the oven on to 325°F. Brush the 8-inch square baking pan with the oil; set the pan aside.

2. Put the eggs, oil, sugar, and salt in the large bowl. With the electric mixer set on medium speed, beat until the mixture is blended. Slowly beat in the cocoa powder. Turn the mixer off. Scrape down the sides of the bowl well with the rubber spatula. Add the cake meal. Turn the mixer on to medium and beat until blended. Turn the mixer off. With the spatula, stir the chocolate chips into the batter.

3. With the spatula, scrape the mixture out of the bowl into the prepared pan. Place the pan on the center rack in the preheated oven. Bake until the brownies are set, 20 to 25 minutes. To test, insert the toothpick into the center; it should come out clean.

4. Put the cooling rack on your counter. Using pot holders, remove the pan from the oven and put it on the cooling rack. Let the brownies cool completely in the pan.

5. When cool, using the knife, cut the pan of brownies into 16 squares. Transfer to the serving plate and dust with confectioners' sugar, if you like, then serve.

NUTRITIONAL ANALYSIS PER BROWNIE: Calories 170 (Kilojoules 714); Protein 2 g; Carbohydrates 21 g; Total Fat 10 g; Saturated Fat 2 g; Cholesterol 27 mg; Sodium 44 mg; Dietary Fiber 0 g

Naturally Perfect Easter Eggs

COOKING TIME: 30 MINUTES

INGREDIENTS

a few fresh carrot tops, celery
    leaves, or flat-leaf parsley leaves

6 eggs

2 cups yellow or red onion skins

vegetable oil

EQUIPMENT

measuring cup

cheesecloth

ruler

kitchen string

scissors

medium saucepan with lid

slotted spoon

pot holder

large bowl

paper towels

PREP TIP: About 3 pounds of onions
yield 2 cups of onion skins. Rub your
hands over each onion to remove the
thin, dry skins. They should slip off.
Save the onions for another use.

Before commercial dyes were available, roots, leaves, and berries were used for dyeing Easter eggs. You can have fun by going back to the basics, using onion skins to color the cooking water and small leaves to make attractive designs.

MAKES 6 EGGS

1. Rinse the carrot, celery, or parsley leaves under cold running water. Shake lightly to remove excess water. Arrange a few wet leaves on 1 egg. Carefully put the leaf-coated egg on a 6-inch square of cheesecloth large enough to cover the egg completely with a little overhang. Holding the leaves in place, wrap the cheesecloth tightly around the egg. (It may be easier to wrap the egg if you first dampen the cheesecloth.) Gather together the ends of the cheesecloth at one end of the egg. Twist together and tie securely with kitchen string. Trim off excess cheesecloth and string with the scissors. Repeat with the remaining 5 eggs.

2. Put the cheesecloth-covered eggs in the medium saucepan. It should be large enough to hold them in a single layer in the bottom without touching. Add cold water to the pan to cover the eggs by 1 inch.

3. Put the onion skins in the saucepan and gently poke them into the water with the slotted spoon. Set the pan on your stove and turn the heat on to high. Bring the water to a boil. As soon as it boils, turn off the heat. Cover the pan and let the eggs sit for 15 minutes.

4. After 15 minutes, using the pot holder, take off the lid, lifting it away from you so that the steam won't burn you. With the slotted spoon, transfer the eggs to the large bowl. Set the bowl in the sink under cold running water until the eggs are cool to the touch, about 2 minutes.

5. Remove the eggs from the water. With the scissors, snip the string and unwrap the cheesecloth. Remove the leaves. Wipe the eggs dry with paper towels.

6. With a paper towel, rub a little vegetable oil on each egg to give it a shine. Store the eggs in the refrigerator for up to 3 days.

NUTRITIONAL ANALYSIS PER EGG: Calories 78 (Kilojoules 328); Protein 6 g; Carbohydrates 1 g; Total Fat 5 g; Saturated Fat 2 g; Cholesterol 213 mg; Sodium 62 mg; Dietary Fiber 0 g

Springtime Asparagus

COOKING TIME: 15 MINUTES

INGREDIENTS

20 asparagus spears, all the same size

about 1 teaspoon salt

3 tablespoons unsalted butter

1 lemon, cut into quarters (optional)

EQUIPMENT

measuring spoons

vegetable peeler

kitchen string

wide, shallow saucepan (make sure the pan is wide enough to hold the asparagus)

metal tongs

small, sharp knife

cloth napkin or paper towels

serving plate

scissors

small saucepan

COOKING TIP: Watch the asparagus spears carefully while they cook. They will turn from bright green to deep, rich dark green to yellow green. They are perfect when they are dark green, and overcooked when they turn yellow green.

Asparagus is one of the first green vegetables to shoot up in early spring, making it a favorite choice for Easter dinner. If you like, sprinkle the asparagus with a little chopped parsley or squeeze a bit of lemon juice on top.

SERVES 4

1. Prepare the asparagus for cooking: Usually an asparagus spear has a tough, fibrous base that is not good to eat. To remove the base, hold the spear at the middle with one hand and the tough end in the other hand. Bend the stalk and it will snap into two parts; the break will be just above the tough base. Throw the base away. If the asparagus is young, slender, and very fresh, it does not need to be peeled. If the asparagus is mature and thick, peeling its tough skin will make it more tender. To peel the asparagus, put 1 spear at a time on a work surface and peel with the vegetable peeler, moving about 1 inch below the tip of the spear down to the base and turning the spear as you work.

2. Gather the asparagus into 4 bundles of 5 spears each. Tie each bundle together with kitchen string. (The bundles make it easy to remove the asparagus from the boiling water.) Set the bundles aside.

3. Fill the wide, shallow saucepan three-fourths full with water. Set the pan on your stove and turn the heat on to high. Bring the water to a rapid boil, then add the salt. (A rapid boil is when the bubbles are big, they rise to the surface quickly, and they break apart immediately.)

4. Using the metal tongs, carefully lower the asparagus bundles into the boiling water. Boil the asparagus, uncovered, until tender when poked with the small, sharp knife and the color is a deep, rich green, about 7 minutes after the water returns to a boil.

5. Carefully lift the cooked asparagus bundles from the water with the metal tongs. Put them on the napkin or paper towels to drain for a few seconds, then transfer to the serving plate. Cut the string with the scissors and throw the string away.

6. Put the butter in the small saucepan. Set the pan on your stove, turn the heat on to low, and melt the butter. Turn off the heat. Pour the butter over the top of the asparagus and serve with the lemon, if you like.

NUTRITIONAL ANALYSIS PER SERVING: Calories 92 (Kilojoules 386); Protein 2 g; Carbohydrates 3 g; Total Fat 9 g; Saturated Fat 5 g; Cholesterol 23 mg; Sodium 3 mg; Dietary Fiber 1 g

Coconut Meringue Nests

COOKING TIME: 2½ HOURS

INGREDIENTS

3 egg whites, at room temperature

¼ teaspoon cream of tartar

pinch of salt

¾ cup granulated sugar

1 teaspoon vanilla extract

about ½ cup shredded coconut

1 package (13 ounces) large jelly
   beans, all different colors

EQUIPMENT

measuring cups and spoons

2 baking sheets

parchment paper

large mixing bowl

electric mixer

rubber spatula

large spoon or table knife

cooling racks

pot holders

serving tray

PREP TIP: Be sure the egg whites are
free of all yolk. If even a tiny bit is
present, they will not beat well.

Meringue is a mixture of egg whites and sugar. Depending upon the proportion of whites to sugar, the meringue can be soft like the top of a lemon meringue pie or crisp like a cookie. This recipe makes the cookie type for a special Easter sweet.

MAKES 12 NESTS

1. Adjust 2 oven racks to be in the center of your oven. Turn the oven on to 225°F. Cover the 2 baking sheets with parchment paper. Set the sheets aside.

2. Put the egg whites in the large mixing bowl. With the electric mixer set on low speed, beat until foamy. Add the cream of tartar and salt. Turn the mixer speed to high and beat until the whites stand in soft peaks when you lift the beaters. (Turn the mixer off before lifting the beaters. They should pull the whites into soft peaks that droop slightly on top.) Turn the mixer to high speed and beat in the sugar 1 tablespoon at a time. Occasionally stop the mixer and scrape the sides of the bowl with the rubber spatula. Continue beating until the whites stand in stiff peaks (no droops) when you lift the beaters. This step will take 15 to 20 minutes. Add the vanilla and beat until blended.

3. With the large spoon, drop 6 equal-sized mounds of the mixture on each baking sheet, leaving plenty of empty space around each mound. With the back of the spoon, make a depression in the center of each mound so that it looks like a little bird's nest. (Or flatten the mound with a table knife, and then raise the sides into a nest shape.) The nests don't have to be perfect. Sprinkle each nest with the coconut. Drop 3 jelly beans into the center of each nest.

4. Place the baking sheets on the center racks in the preheated oven. Bake the nests for 2 hours. Turn off the oven and let the nests sit in the warm turned-off oven for 30 minutes.

5. Put the cooling racks on your counter. Using pot holders, remove the baking sheets and place on the racks. Let the nests cool completely.

6. With your fingers, carefully peel each nest from the paper. Put the nests on the serving tray. Add a few more jelly beans to the center of each nest.

NUTRITIONAL ANALYSIS PER NEST: Calories 68 (Kilojoules 286); Protein 1 g; Carbohydrates 14 g; Total Fat 1 g; Saturated Fat 1 g; Cholesterol 0 mg; Sodium 33 mg; Dietary Fiber 0 g

Buttermilk Biscuits

COOKING TIME: 15 MINUTES

INGREDIENTS

2 cups all-purpose flour

1 tablespoon baking powder

2 teaspoons granulated sugar

½ teaspoon salt

¼ teaspoon baking soda

5½ tablespoons solid vegetable shortening

1 cup buttermilk

flour for shaping and cutting dough

EQUIPMENT

measuring cups and spoons

fine-mesh sieve

medium mixing bowl

mixing spoon

table fork

2½-inch biscuit cutter

metal spatula

baking sheet

cooling rack

pot holders

Biscuits are called "quick" breads because they are made with baking powder or baking soda instead of yeast, which means they are easy and quick to make. Eat them warm with butter and jam or honey for Easter breakfast, or split them and use them for making sandwiches with leftover Easter ham.

MAKES 12 BISCUITS

1. Adjust a rack to be in the center of your oven without another rack above it. Turn the oven on to 450°F.

2. To sift the dry ingredients: Set the fine-mesh sieve over the mixing bowl. Put the flour (a little at a time), baking powder, sugar, salt, and baking soda into the sieve and press it through the sieve with the back of the mixing spoon. Stir lightly with the spoon to mix. Add the shortening and rub it gently into the dry ingredients with your fingertips until the mixture looks like coarse crumbs.

3. Add the buttermilk and stir with the fork just until a soft dough forms.

4. With your fingers, lightly sprinkle a flat work surface with flour. Turn the dough out of the bowl onto the floured surface. With your fingertips, knead the dough gently until smooth, about 12 turns.

5. With your hand, pat the dough into a ½-inch-thick circle. Dip the biscuit cutter in flour. Holding the biscuit cutter firmly, press it straight down into the dough to cut out as many rounds as you can. Using the spatula, transfer the biscuits to the ungreased baking sheet, spacing them 1 inch apart.

6. Very gently push the dough scraps together and pat out to a round ½ inch thick. Cut out more biscuits. Repeat until all the dough has been cut.

7. Place the baking sheet on the center rack in the preheated oven. Bake the biscuits until they are a light golden brown, 12 to 15 minutes.

8. Put the cooling rack on your counter. Using pot holders, remove the baking sheet from the oven and put it on the cooling rack. Let the biscuits cool slightly, about 3 minutes. With the spatula, remove the biscuits from the baking sheet. Serve hot.

NUTRITIONAL ANALYSIS PER BISCUIT: Calories 144 (Kilojoules 605); Protein 3 g; Carbohydrates 19 g; Total Fat 6 g; Saturated Fat 2 g; Cholesterol 1 mg; Sodium 266 mg; Dietary Fiber 1 g

Strawberry Tartlets

COOKING TIME: 12 MINUTES

INGREDIENTS

1 recipe Basic Pie Pastry *(page 16)*

3 to 4 cups small, ripe strawberries

¼ cup red currant jelly

1 teaspoon granulated sugar

½ recipe Sweetened Whipped Cream *(page 18)*

EQUIPMENT

measuring cups and spoons

six ¾-cup custard cups

baking sheet

small, sharp knife

table fork

cooling rack

pot holders

serving plate

cutting board

small saucepan

wooden spoon

hot pad

small spoon

SAFETY TIP: Ask an adult for help when it comes time to melt the jelly and sugar.

Here, strawberries are arranged in individual pastry shells for a special springtime dessert. If you have a 5-inch scalloped (or plain) round cookie cutter, use it instead of the small, sharp knife to cut out the rounds of pastry.

MAKES 6 TARTLETS

1. Prepare the pie pastry dough and roll out as directed. Adjust an oven rack to be in the center of your oven without another rack above it. Turn the oven on to 450°F. Put the 6 custard cups upside down on the baking sheet. Using the open end of a custard cup as a guide, cut out 6 dough rounds with the knife, making them about ¼ inch larger than the cup rim. Put each dough round on the back of a custard cup, pressing gently to fit it around the cup. (You may need to gather dough scraps together and reroll to cut all 6 rounds.) With the fork, prick holes all over the bottom and sides of the dough. (Pricking the dough with the tines of a fork helps to keep its shape while baking.)

2. Place the baking sheet on the center rack in the preheated oven. Bake until the shells are golden brown, 10 to 12 minutes.

3. Put the cooling rack on your counter. Using pot holders, transfer the baking sheet to the rack. Let the shells cool completely.

4. With your fingers, lift the cooled shells from the cups and set them, open end up, on the serving plate.

5. Put the strawberries on the cutting board. With the small, sharp knife, remove the green stems from the berries.

6. Put the jelly and sugar in the small saucepan. Set the pan on your stove and turn the heat on to medium. Stirring often with the wooden spoon, heat until the jelly melts and comes to a boil, about 2 minutes. Then, without stirring, boil for 1 minute. Put the hot pad on your counter. Using pot holders, put the pan on the hot pad. Let cool slightly.

7. Fill each shell with the berries, placing them pointed ends up. With the spoon, drizzle a little melted jelly over the berries. Make the whipped cream. Spoon some whipped cream onto each tartlet and serve.

NUTRITIONAL ANALYSIS PER TARTLET: Calories 370 (Kilojoules 1,554); Protein 3 g; Carbohydrates 39 g; Total Fat 23 g; Saturated Fat 8 g; Cholesterol 27 mg; Sodium 206 mg; Dietary Fiber 3 g

Soft-Cooked Eggs

COOKING TIME: 10 MINUTES

INGREDIENTS

2 eggs

salt and ground pepper to taste

EQUIPMENT

small saucepan

large slotted spoon

2 egg cups

SERVING TIP: To eat a soft-cooked egg, lightly crack the shell around the top third of the egg with a table knife. Cut the top off of the egg with the knife. Sprinkle salt and pepper over the egg, and then eat the egg directly from the shell with a spoon.

Soft-cooked eggs make the perfect centerpiece for a special Mother's Day breakfast. Put the eggs on a tray along with some fruit salad (page 45) and a raisin scone (page 47) and serve your mom breakfast in bed. To make the egg more festive, dye the outside a pretty color by adding 1 teaspoon distilled white vinegar and 1 teaspoon food coloring of choice to the cooking water.

SERVES 1

1. Place the eggs in the small saucepan. (Put them in a pan just large enough to hold them in a single layer.) Pour in water to cover the eggs by 1 inch. If the eggs are at room temperature, use lukewarm water. If the eggs are cold, use cold water.

2. Put the pan, uncovered, on a burner of your stove and turn the heat on to medium. Let the water come just to a boil, then reduce the heat so that bubbles in the water barely reach the surface. Immediately set the timer. How long the eggs should cook depends upon personal taste and the size, freshness, and temperature of the eggs. In 3¾ minutes, a large, fresh, room-temperature egg should cook so that the white is starting to turn jellylike, but the yolk is still runny. In 5½ minutes, the white should be almost solid and the yolk beginning to set. Think about the way your mom likes her eggs and set the timer accordingly. (Cooking the eggs 4½ minutes is a pretty safe bet.) Of course, if you let the water boil, the eggs will cook faster, so keep the water at a simmer.

3. When the eggs are cooked, carefully lift them from the water with the large slotted spoon. Place them, large end up, in the egg cups. Serve immediately with salt and pepper.

NUTRITIONAL ANALYSIS PER SERVING: Calories 149 (Kilojoules 626); Protein 12 g; Carbohydrates 1 g; Total Fat 10 g; Saturated Fat 3 g; Cholesterol 425 mg; Sodium 126 mg; Dietary Fiber 0 g

Melon and Berry Fruit Bowl

INGREDIENTS

1 cantaloupe

4 large, perfect strawberries

5 perfect raspberries

1 or 2 fresh mint sprigs

EQUIPMENT

cutting board

large, sharp knife

table spoon

aluminum foil or plastic wrap

melon baller

medium mixing bowl

small, sharp knife

mixing spoon

serving bowl

Moms are sure to love this special springtime fruit salad—especially when served on Mother's Day. Take a little extra care to make it as pretty as possible, arranging the fruit just so and garnishing with a mint sprig.

SERVES 1

1. Put the cantaloupe on the cutting board with the stem end up. With the large, sharp knife, cut the cantaloupe in half vertically. With the spoon, scrape the seeds from the cantaloupe halves and discard them. Wrap one-half of the cantaloupe in aluminum foil or plastic wrap and refrigerate it for another use. With the melon baller, scoop out a ball-shaped piece of melon by turning the melon baller all the way around the spoonful of fruit. Repeat to make as many melon balls as you can. Place the melon balls in the medium bowl. Set the bowl aside.

2. Put the strawberries on the cutting board. With the small, sharp knife, remove the green stems from the strawberries. Still using the small knife, cut the strawberries lengthwise into slices. Add the strawberries to the cantaloupe balls along with the raspberries. Mix gently.

3. Pile the melon balls, strawberries, and raspberries in the serving bowl. Garnish with the mint sprigs. If you are not serving the fruit immediately, cover the bowl with plastic wrap and refrigerate it until you are ready to serve.

NUTRITIONAL ANALYSIS PER SERVING: Calories 37 (Kilojoules 155); Protein 1 g; Carbohydrates 9 g; Total Fat 0 g; Saturated Fat 0 g; Cholesterol 0 mg; Sodium 6 mg; Dietary Fiber 2 g

Raisin Scones

COOKING TIME: 10 MINUTES

INGREDIENTS

about 2 cups all-purpose flour

3 tablespoons granulated sugar

1 tablespoon baking powder

½ teaspoon salt

¼ cup unsalted butter, chilled

⅓ cup seedless golden raisins

1 egg

⅓ cup milk

flour for kneading dough

1 to 2 tablespoons milk for brushing tops of scones

granulated sugar for sprinkling tops of scones

butter, jam, or honey for serving (optional)

EQUIPMENT

measuring cups and spoons

fine-mesh sieve

medium mixing bowl

mixing spoon

small mixing bowl

table fork

sharp knife

ruler

pastry brush

baking sheet

cooling rack

pot holders

metal spatula

Pop one of these scones onto mom's Mother's Day breakfast tray and pass out the rest, still piping hot, to family and friends. They are also a wonderful morning treat on any other day of the year. If you like, substitute currants or pecans for the raisins.

MAKES 12 SCONES

1. Adjust an oven rack to be in the center of your oven without another rack above it. Turn the oven on to 450°F.

2. To sift the flour: Set the fine-mesh sieve over a measuring cup. Put the flour into the sieve, a little at a time, and press through with the back of the spoon. You will need 2 cups sifted flour.

3. Put the flour, sugar, baking powder, and salt into the medium bowl. Cut the butter into pieces. Add it to the flour mixture and mix gently with your fingertips until the mixture looks like coarse crumbs. With the spoon, gently stir in the raisins.

4. Break the egg into the small bowl. Add the milk and beat with the fork until the mixture is well blended. Pour the egg mixture over the flour mixture. Stir lightly with the fork until the mixture comes together.

5. Lightly sprinkle a flat work surface with flour. Turn the mixture out of the bowl onto the floured surface. Knead lightly until the mixture forms a smooth dough. Cut the dough in half with the sharp knife. Lightly and gently pat each half into a 6-inch circle. With the pastry brush, brush the top of each round with the milk. Then sprinkle the tops with the sugar. With the sharp knife, cut each circle into 6 wedges. Place the wedges, 1 inch apart, on the ungreased baking sheet.

6. Place the baking sheet in the center of the preheated oven. Bake until the scones are light golden brown, about 10 minutes.

7. Put the cooling rack on your counter. Using pot holders, remove the baking sheet from the oven and put it on the cooling rack. Let the scones cool slightly, about 3 minutes. With the spatula, remove the scones from the baking sheets. Serve hot with butter, jam, or honey, if desired.

NUTRITIONAL ANALYSIS PER SCONE: Calories 151 (Kilojoules 634); Protein 3 g; Carbohydrates 24 g; Total Fat 5 g; Saturated Fat 3 g; Cholesterol 29 mg; Sodium 229 mg; Dietary Fiber 1 g

Frozen Fruit Pops

INGREDIENTS

5 large, ripe strawberries

1 banana

1 cup plain yogurt

½ cup applesauce

¼ cup apple juice

1 tablespoon honey

EQUIPMENT

measuring cups and spoons

cutting board

small, sharp knife

medium mixing bowl

mixing spoon

five 5-ounce paper cups

aluminum foil

5 wooden ice-cream sticks

These frozen pops are the coolest treats going. Dad might get a bang out of them, too, especially on Father's Day.

MAKES 5 POPS

1. Put the strawberries on the cutting board. With the small, sharp knife, remove the green stems from the berries. Chop the strawberries into small pieces. Put the pieces in the medium bowl.

2. Peel the banana and put it on the cutting board. With the small, sharp knife, chop the banana. Add the chopped banana to the strawberries in the bowl.

3. Add the yogurt, applesauce, apple juice, and honey to the fruit in the bowl. With the spoon, stir well to combine the ingredients.

4. Spoon the mixture into the five 5-ounce paper cups, dividing the mixture evenly among the cups.

5. Cover each cup with aluminum foil. Make a hole in the center of each piece of foil and insert a wooden stick through the hole down the center of the mixture to the bottom of the cup.

6. Set the cups in the freezer. Freeze until the pops are completely frozen, about 4 hours. To serve, remove the foil and peel off the paper cup. Enjoy.

NUTRITIONAL ANALYSIS PER POP: Calories 81 (Kilojoules 340); Protein 3 g; Carbohydrates 17 g; Total Fat 1 g; Saturated Fat 0 g; Cholesterol 3 mg; Sodium 33 mg; Dietary Fiber 1 g

Favorite Potato Salad

COOKING TIME: 25 MINUTES

INGREDIENTS

15 small red-skinned potatoes,
about 2 pounds total weight

about ¾ teaspoon salt

2 tablespoons olive oil

1 tablespoon vinegar

1 teaspoon mustard

2 celery stalks

1 red bell pepper

½ cup mayonnaise

¼ cup sour cream

½ teaspoon celery seeds

EQUIPMENT

measuring cups and spoons

large saucepan

table fork

colander

small cup

cutting board

small, sharp knife

large mixing bowl

mixing spoon

medium mixing bowl

plastic wrap

serving bowl

This old-fashioned potato salad is sure to please on Father's Day. Use potatoes about 2 inches in diameter.

SERVES 8

1. Put the potatoes in the large saucepan. Pour in enough cold water to cover the potatoes by 1 inch. Add ½ teaspoon of the salt. Set the pan on your stove, turn the heat on to high, and bring the water to a rapid boil. Then reduce the heat so that the potatoes boil gently. Cook, uncovered, until the potatoes are tender when pierced with the fork, 20 to 25 minutes.

2. Put the colander in your sink. Ask an adult to pour the potatoes and water into the colander, letting the water drain away in the sink. Set the potatoes aside until they are cool enough to handle, 15 to 20 minutes.

3. Put the oil, vinegar, and mustard in the small cup. Beat with the fork until the mixture is combined; set aside.

4. Place the potatoes on the cutting board. With the small, sharp knife, cut each warm potato into large bite-sized chunks. Put the chunks in the large mixing bowl. Sprinkle the potatoes with the vinegar-oil mixture. With the spoon, mix gently. Set aside for 15 minutes.

5. Put the celery stalks on the cutting board. With the small, sharp knife, trim off the ends of the celery stalks, then dice the stalks. Put the celery in the medium bowl. Put the bell pepper on the cutting board. With the small, sharp knife, cut lengthwise to remove a quarter of the bell pepper. Wrap the large piece in plastic wrap and reserve for another use. With your fingers, remove the stem, seeds, and ribs from the quarter, then dice the pepper and add to the celery.

6. Add the mayonnaise, sour cream, celery seeds, and the remaining ¼ teaspoon salt to the celery and the red pepper. Stir well with the spoon. Spoon the mixture over the potatoes. Gently mix the potatoes with the mayonnaise mixture until they are evenly coated. Taste and add more salt, if necessary. Transfer the salad to the serving bowl. Cover the bowl with plastic wrap and refrigerate until well chilled, about 1 hour.

7. Serve the salad chilled. Just before serving, taste to see if it needs more salt.

NUTRITIONAL ANALYSIS PER SERVING: Calories 241 (Kilojoules 1,012); Protein 3 g; Carbohydrates 22 g; Total Fat 16 g; Saturated Fat 3 g; Cholesterol 11 mg; Sodium 326 mg; Dietary Fiber 2 g

Hero Sandwiches

INGREDIENTS

4 crusty French or Italian rolls,
   each 5 to 6 inches long

¼ cup olive oil

I tablespoon red wine vinegar

I teaspoon dried oregano

2 tablespoons grated Parmesan
   cheese

¼ pound thinly sliced Genoa salami

¼ pound thinly sliced mortadella
   or bologna

¼ pound thinly sliced provolone
   cheese

I large, firm tomato

about ⅓ head iceberg lettuce

4 teaspoons chopped pimiento

EQUIPMENT

measuring cups and spoons

cutting board

serrated bread knife

paring knife

large, sharp knife

aluminum foil or plastic wrap,
   if needed

SERVING TIP: Use a serrated bread
knife, which has a toothed-edge
blade, to cut the sandwiches in half.
It neatly cuts through foods with
tough shells and soft interiors (like
crusty bread and ripe tomatoes).

Make a hero for your hero on Father's Day. The sandwiches
are also good to take on picnics or to pack in a lunch box for a
special treat.

MAKES 4 SANDWICHES

1. Put the rolls on the cutting board. With the serrated bread knife, cut
each roll in half horizontally.

2. Sprinkle the olive oil, vinegar, oregano, and Parmesan cheese over
the cut surface of each roll half, dividing the ingredients evenly among
the halves.

3. Arrange layers of Genoa salami and mortadella or bologna over the
bottom half of each roll, giving each bottom half an equal amount of
each meat. If necessary, cut the meat slices to make sure that they fit
the bread and are evenly divided among the sandwiches. Top with the
cheese slices, again giving each sandwich an equal amount of cheese.

4. Put the tomato on the cutting board. With the paring knife, cut
out the stem end. Steady the tomato and, with the serrated knife, cut
into 8 slices. Put 2 slices of tomato over the meat on the bottom half
of each roll.

5. Put the lettuce on the cutting board. With the large, sharp knife, cut
the lettuce into thin strips. You should have about 1⅓ cups. Put about
⅓ cup lettuce strips over the tomato slices on the bottom half of each roll.

6. Sprinkle I teaspoon chopped pimiento over the lettuce on the bottom
half of each roll.

7. Set the top half of each roll over the ingredients on the bottom half to
make sandwiches and serve immediately. Or wrap each sandwich tightly
in aluminum foil or plastic wrap and refrigerate until ready to serve.

NUTRITIONAL ANALYSIS PER SANDWICH: Calories 617 (Kilojoules 2,591); Protein 26 g;
Carbohydrates 39 g; Total Fat 40 g; Saturated Fat 14 g; Cholesterol 67 mg; Sodium 1,548 mg;
Dietary Fiber 3 g

Red, White, and Blueberry Bowl

Start the Fourth of July with a bang by making an all-American red, white, and blueberry breakfast. It is certain to win compliments. You can make one big bowl or individual servings.

SERVES 4

1. Put the blueberries in a pretty glass serving bowl or divide evenly among 4 individual glass bowls.

2. Put the strawberries on the cutting board. With the small, sharp knife, remove the green stems from the strawberries. Put the strawberries in the bowl or bowls with the blueberries.

3. Peel the bananas. Put the bananas on the cutting board. With the knife, cut each banana into ½-inch-thick rounds. Add the banana rounds to the berries. Mix the fruit gently with the spoon.

4. Spoon the yogurt on top of the fruit. Sprinkle the brown sugar and then the granola over the yogurt. Serve immediately.

NUTRITIONAL ANALYSIS PER SERVING: Calories 324 (Kilojoules 1,361); Protein 10 g; Carbohydrates 55 g; Total Fat 8 g; Saturated Fat 4 g; Cholesterol 7 mg; Sodium 97 mg; Dietary Fiber 5 g

INGREDIENTS

½ pint blueberries

20 large strawberries

2 large bananas

2 cups plain yogurt

2 tablespoons dark brown sugar

1 cup granola

EQUIPMENT

measuring cups

clear glass serving bowl or 4 individual glass bowls

cutting board

small, sharp knife

mixing spoon

PREP TIP: Choose plump and somewhat firm strawberries and blueberries. They will hold up best when the mixture is stirred.

Chicken and Vegetable Kabobs

COOKING TIME: 20 MINUTES

INGREDIENTS

1 small yellow or red bell pepper

1 small red onion

1 small lemon

⅓ cup olive oil

1 large garlic clove

¼ teaspoon ground cumin

¼ teaspoon dried thyme

¼ teaspoon salt

⅛ teaspoon pepper

4 boneless, skinless chicken breast
   halves

EQUIPMENT

measuring cups and spoons

cutting board

small, sharp knife

large glass bowl

garlic press

table fork

mixing spoon

4 long metal skewers

broiler pan

pastry brush

pot holders, metal tongs, and
   hot pad

SAFETY TIP: Ask an adult for help
when it comes time to use the broiler.

1. Put the bell pepper on the cutting board. With the small, sharp knife, cut the pepper in half lengthwise. With your fingers, remove the stem, seeds, and ribs from each half. Cut each pepper half into 4 equal chunks.

2. Put the onion on the cutting board. With the knife, cut in half from the root to the stem end. Place the halves, flat side down, on the cutting board and cut off a thin slice from each root and stem end. Pull off the papery skin. Cut each onion half into 4 equal chunks.

3. Make the marinade: Put the lemon on the cutting board. With the knife, cut the lemon in half crosswise. Squeeze the juice from each half into the large glass bowl. Add the olive oil. Put the garlic clove on the cutting board. Hit with the side of the garlic press. Pull off the skin, then press the garlic through the press into the bowl. Add the cumin, thyme, salt, and pepper. Stir with the fork until mixed. Set aside.

4. Put the chicken breasts on the cutting board. With the small, sharp knife, cut each chicken breast half lengthwise into 4 strips. Put in the bowl with the marinade. With the spoon, stir to coat the chicken.

5. Adjust a broiler rack so the top of the broiler pan will be 4 to 6 inches from the source of the heat. Turn the broiler on to high.

6. Remove the chicken from the marinade. Reserve the marinade. Divide the chicken and the vegetables into 4 equal portions. Thread the portions, alternating the chicken pieces with the vegetable pieces, onto the 4 skewers. Snake each chicken strip through the skewer 2 or 3 times. Do not pack the foods too tightly.

7. Place the skewers on the broiler pan. With the pastry brush, brush the kabobs with the leftover marinade. Carefully set the broiler pan under the broiler and broil the kabobs until browned on one side, 5 to 10 minutes. Using pot holders, carefully pull out the broiler rack a little. With the metal tongs, turn each kabob over. Push the pan back under the broiler and broil the kabobs until browned on the second side, 5 to 10 minutes.

8. Put the hot pad on your counter. Using pot holders, remove the pan from the broiler and set it on the hot pad. Serve the kabobs immediately.

NUTRITIONAL ANALYSIS PER SERVING: Calories 302 (Kilojoules 1,268); Protein 27 g; Carbohydrates 4 g; Total Fat 19 g; Saturated Fat 3 g; Cholesterol 66 mg; Sodium 221 mg; Dietary Fiber 1 g

Patriotic Nachos

INGREDIENTS

FOR THE SALSA

6 small, ripe plum tomatoes

1 or 2 green onions

1 small lime

6 fresh cilantro sprigs or 2 fresh
  flat-leaf parsley sprigs

1 tablespoon well-drained canned
  diced green chile (optional)

½ teaspoon ground cumin

½ teaspoon salt

FOR THE NACHOS

4 to 5 cups blue corn chips (4 to
  6 ounces)

1 tablespoon well-drained canned
  diced green chile

2 cups (8 ounces) shredded
  Monterey jack cheese

EQUIPMENT

measuring cups and spoons

cutting board

small, sharp knife

medium mixing bowl

mixing spoon

9-by-13-inch flameproof baking dish

hot pad and pot holders

small serving bowl

metal spatula, if needed

serving plate, if using

SAFETY TIP: Ask an adult for help
when it comes time to use the broiler.

SERVES 4

1. First, make the salsa: Put the tomatoes on the cutting board. With the small, sharp knife, cut each tomato in half lengthwise. Put each tomato half, cut side down, on the cutting board. Cut out the cores and chop the tomatoes into very small pieces. Put into the medium bowl. Put the green onion on the cutting board. With the small, sharp knife, cut off the root and peel off the outer layer of skin. Cut off the dark leaves about 3 inches above the white root end. Cut the pieces of white and pale green leaves into thin slices. Add to the tomatoes in the mixing bowl.

2. Put the lime on the cutting board. With the knife, cut the lime in half crosswise. Reserve one half for another use. Squeeze the juice from the remaining half and add it to the tomato mixture.

3. With your fingers, remove the cilantro or parsley leaves from the stems. Put the leaves on the cutting board. With the knife, finely chop the leaves. Add the chopped leaves to the tomato mixture.

4. Add the chile (if using), cumin, and salt. Stir with the spoon until well mixed. Taste the salsa and add more lime juice or salt if you think it needs it. Set the salsa aside.

5. Now, make the nachos: Adjust a broiler rack so it is about 6 inches from the source of the heat. Turn the broiler on to high.

6. Spread the chips over the bottom of the flameproof baking dish. Sprinkle the chips evenly with the diced chile. (Use more chile if you like hot nachos. Use less if you like milder nachos.) Then sprinkle with the shredded cheese. Using a total of ¼ cup of the salsa, put little dabs of the salsa over the cheese.

7. Set the dish under the broiler and heat just until the cheese melts, about 4 minutes. Watch carefully, as the cheese melts quickly.

8. Put the hot pad on your counter. Using pot holders, carefully remove the dish from the broiler and put it on the hot pad. Let the nachos sit until they are cool enough to touch, about 3 minutes.

9. Put the salsa in the small serving bowl. Serve the warm nachos from the baking dish or, using the metal spatula, transfer them to the serving plate.

NUTRITIONAL ANALYSIS PER SERVING: Calories 416 (Kilojoules 1,747); Protein 18 g; Carbohydrates 28 g; Total Fat 26 g; Saturated Fat 11 g; Cholesterol 60 mg; Sodium 670 mg; Dietary Fiber 3 g

Butter-Roasted Corn on the Cob

COOKING TIME: 30 MINUTES

INGREDIENTS

4 ears of corn

3 tablespoons unsalted butter, softened

½ teaspoon dried marjoram

¼ teaspoon salt

big pinch of ground pepper

EQUIPMENT

measuring spoons

vegetable brush

paper towels

small bowl

table fork

4 sheets aluminum foil (about 12 inches square)

table knife

metal tongs

serving platter

COOKING TIP: If an adult is lighting a charcoal fire in the grill, offer to prepare the corn, and then let them cook the ears over the fire.

Thomas Jefferson was the principal author of the Declaration of Independence and the third president of the United States. He was also America's first noted gourmet. (A gourmet is a person who loves good food.) He introduced Americans to foreign foods and foreigners to American foods. When he was minister to France, Jefferson astounded his French guests by serving corn on the cob. You can pay a personal tribute to Jefferson on the Fourth of July by serving the same delicious treat.

SERVES 4

1. Adjust an oven rack to be in the center of your oven without another rack above it. Turn the oven on to 325°F.

2. Pull off the husk from around each ear of corn. With the dry vegetable brush, brush away the silk (the threads) from between the kernel rows. Rinse the husked corn under cold running water, drain, and dry well with paper towels.

3. Put the butter, marjoram, salt, and pepper in the small bowl. Beat with the fork until the ingredients are well combined. Put the 4 sheets of aluminum foil on your counter. Set 1 ear of corn on each piece of foil. With the table knife, spread the seasoned butter over each ear of corn, dividing the butter equally among the 4 ears. Wrap each ear of corn in its piece of foil. Be careful not to leave any open spaces.

4. Place the wrapped corn on the rack in the preheated oven. Roast the corn for 15 minutes. With the metal tongs, turn each ear of corn over. Roast the corn 15 minutes longer. The corn should cook about 30 minutes in all, but if it cooks a little more it will still be good.

5. Using the tongs, remove the ears of corn from the oven and put them on the serving platter. Serve the corn immediately, unwrapping and removing the hot foil carefully.

NUTRITIONAL ANALYSIS PER SERVING: Calories 154 (Kilojoules 647); Protein 3 g; Carbohydrates 17 g; Total Fat 10 g; Saturated Fat 6 g; Cholesterol 23 mg; Sodium 158 mg; Dietary Fiber 3 g

Halloween Spice Cookies

INGREDIENTS

shortening for greasing baking sheets

1 medium carrot

½ cup each all-purpose flour and
rolled oats

1½ teaspoons baking powder

½ teaspoon ground cinnamon

⅛ teaspoon ground cloves

pinch of salt

½ cup firmly packed dark brown sugar

¼ cup unsalted butter, at room
temperature

1 egg

1 teaspoon vanilla extract

2 recipes Basic Icing (*page 18*)

green, red, and yellow food coloring

Halloween sprinkles for decorating

EQUIPMENT

measuring cups and spoons

2 baking sheets

cutting board

vegetable peeler, small knife, and
box grater-shredder

medium, large, and small mixing bowls

wooden spoon, electric mixer, and
rubber spatula

hot pads, cooling racks, and pot
holders

metal spatula

small icing spatula or table knife

pastry bag with plain writing tip

MAKES ABOUT 20 COOKIES

1. Adjust 2 oven racks to be in the center of your oven. Turn the oven on to 375°F. Lightly and evenly grease the baking sheets with the shortening. Set them aside.

2. Put the carrot on the cutting board. With the vegetable peeler, peel the carrot. With the small knife, cut off the root and stem ends. Grate the carrot on the large holes of the grater. Set the grated carrot aside. Put the flour, oats, baking powder, cinnamon, cloves, and salt in the medium mixing bowl. Stir with the wooden spoon until mixed. Set the bowl aside.

3. Put the sugar and butter in the large mixing bowl. With the electric mixer set on medium speed, beat until well blended. Add the egg and the vanilla and beat on medium speed until smooth and well blended. Turn off the mixer and scrape the sides of the bowl with the rubber spatula. Turn the mixer on to low speed and gradually beat the flour mixture into the butter mixture. Beat in the grated carrot.

4. Drop rounded tablespoonfuls of the dough onto the prepared baking sheets, spacing them well apart.

5. Place the baking sheets in the preheated oven. Bake until the cookies start to brown, 10 to 12 minutes.

6. Put the hot pads and cooling racks on your counter. Using pot holders, remove the sheets from the oven and put them on the hot pads. Let the cookies sit for 1 minute, then carefully slip the metal spatula under each cookie and transfer it to a rack. Let the cookies cool completely.

7. Make the icing. Spoon about one-third of the icing into the small bowl. Add enough green food coloring to the icing to make it green. Add enough drops of red and yellow food coloring to the rest of the icing to tint it orange.

8. Spread the orange icing over the top of each cookie with the icing spatula or table knife. With the rubber spatula, put the green icing in the pastry bag fitted with the writing tip. Pipe a jack-o'-lantern face on some cookies with some of the green icing. Decorate the rest with the sprinkles.

NUTRITIONAL ANALYSIS PER COOKIE: Calories 133 (Kilojoules 559); Protein 1 g; Carbohydrates 22 g; Total Fat 5 g; Saturated Fat 3 g; Cholesterol 22 mg; Sodium 51 mg; Dietary Fiber 0 g

Spiced Cider

COOKING TIME: 5 MINUTES,
PLUS 30 MINUTES FOR
COOLING

INGREDIENTS

8 cups (2 quarts) unsweetened non-alcoholic apple cider

2 tablespoons honey

12 whole cloves

6 whole allspice

2 cinnamon sticks, each about 3 inches long

1 large orange

1 large apple

EQUIPMENT

measuring cups and spoons

large saucepan

long-handled spoon

sieve

large mixing bowl or pitcher

cutting board

small, sharp knife

8 mugs and spoons

ladle

Halloween is the perfect time of year to serve this festive drink. It can be served warm or cold. To serve the cider cold, strain it as directed in step 2, and then pour into a container. Cover and refrigerate until cold. Then, when it comes time to serve, pour the cold cider into a small punch bowl and add the fruit slices.

SERVES 8

1. Put the apple cider in the large saucepan. Add the honey, cloves, allspice, and cinnamon sticks. Stir with the long-handled spoon to mix the ingredients. Set the pan on your stove, turn the heat on to high, and bring the mixture to a boil. Immediately reduce the heat to medium-low and let the mixture simmer for 5 minutes. Remove the cider from the heat and let cool for 30 minutes.

2. Put the sieve over the large mixing bowl or pitcher. With the help of an adult, pour the cider through the sieve into the bowl or pitcher. Discard the spices in the sieve. Pour the cider back into the saucepan.

3. Turn the heat back on to low and heat the cider until it is warm but not too hot to drink.

4. Steady the orange upright on the cutting board. With the small, sharp knife, cut the orange in half lengthwise. Place the orange halves, flat side down, on the cutting board. Cut each half across into thin half-circle slices. Set the slices aside.

5. Put the apple, stem end up, on the cutting board. With the knife, cut the apple in half. Cut away the stem and core from the apple halves. Place the apple halves, flat side down, on the cutting board. Cut each half across into thin half-circle slices.

6. Divide the orange and apple slices evenly among 8 mugs. Ladle the hot cider into the mugs, dividing evenly. Serve immediately with spoons for scooping up the fruit slices to eat after the cider is gone.

NUTRITIONAL ANALYSIS PER SERVING: Calories 157 (Kilojoules 659); Protein 1 g; Carbohydrates 41 g; Total Fat 0 g; Saturated Fat 0 g; Cholesterol 0 mg; Sodium 9 mg; Dietary Fiber 1 g

Devil's Food Cupcakes

COOKING TIME: 20 MINUTES

INGREDIENTS

1 cup all-purpose flour

2 tablespoons unsweetened cocoa powder

½ teaspoon baking soda

¼ cup unsalted butter, softened

¾ cup granulated sugar

1 egg

½ cup milk

½ teaspoon vanilla extract

¼ teaspoon salt

1 recipe Basic Icing (page 18), made with cocoa powder

1 recipe Basic Icing (page 18), for decorating (optional)

EQUIPMENT

measuring cups and spoons

12 paper cupcake liners

standard 12-cup muffin pan

flour sifter

2 medium mixing bowls

electric mixer

rubber spatula

spoon

2 toothpicks

cooling rack

pot holders

small icing spatula or table knife

1. Adjust an oven rack to be in the center of your oven without another rack above it. Turn the oven on to 350°F. Put the cupcake liners in the muffin cups.

2. Using the flour sifter, sift together the flour, cocoa, and baking soda into a medium bowl; set aside.

3. Put the butter and sugar in the other medium bowl. With the electric mixer set on medium speed, beat the butter and sugar until well blended, about 2 minutes. Turn off the mixer. Add the egg to the bowl. Beat the mixture on medium speed until light and fluffy, about 2 minutes. Turn off the mixer and scrape the sides of the bowl with the rubber spatula. Add half of the flour mixture and beat on medium speed just until the ingredients are combined. Turn off the mixer, scrape the sides of the bowl, and add the milk, vanilla, and salt. Beat the mixture on low speed until blended. Slowly beat in the remaining flour mixture. Beat until the batter is well blended.

4. Spoon the batter into the paper-lined cups, dividing it evenly.

5. Place the muffin pan on the center rack in the preheated oven. Bake the cupcakes until they have risen and are set in the center, 15 to 20 minutes. To test, insert a toothpick into the center of a cupcake. It should come out clean (without any uncooked batter on it).

6. Put the cooling rack on your counter. Using pot holders, remove the muffin pan from the oven and set on the cooling rack. Let the cupcakes cool completely.

7. Make 1 recipe Basic Icing, adding the cocoa powder. To make the spider web design, make a second recipe of Basic Icing, keeping it plain.

8. Remove the cupcakes from the muffin pan. With the icing spatula or table knife, spread the dark icing over the top of each cupcake. To make a spider web design, using the icing spatula or table knife, drizzle 3 rings of white icing on top of the chocolate. Starting in the center with the smallest ring, drag the clean toothpick through the icing. Repeat several times all the way around the cupcake. Set the cupcakes aside until the icing is set, about 30 minutes.

NUTRITIONAL ANALYSIS PER CUPCAKE: Calories 244 (Kilojoules 1,025); Protein 3 g; Carbohydrates 42 g; Total Fat 8 g; Saturated Fat 5 g; Cholesterol 38 mg; Sodium 113 mg; Dietary Fiber 1 g

Caramel Apples

COOKING TIME: 15 MINUTES

INGREDIENTS

6 small, unwaxed apples

1 cup sliced almonds, chopped pecans, granola, cookie crumbs, or shredded coconut for coating apples

1 package (14 ounces) caramels, unwrapped

2 tablespoons water

EQUIPMENT

measuring cups and spoons

6 wooden ice-cream sticks

hot pad

baking sheet

waxed paper

double boiler

wooden spoon

pot holders

PREP TIP: When it comes time to coat the apples with nuts or other coating ingredients, you may need to press the coating on with your fingers to help it stick.

Kids and grown-ups alike will find it hard to resist these Halloween treats. If you wish, you can wrap the apples to share them with your friends. Once the caramel is set, wrap each apple in orange cellophane, and then tie the cellophane with a black licorice whip.

MAKES 6 APPLES

1. Twist the apple stems until they come off. Stick a wooden ice-cream stick into the stem end of each apple until it's firmly inserted. Set the apples aside.

2. Put the hot pad on your kitchen counter. Put the baking sheet near the hot pad and line it with a sheet of waxed paper. Divide the nuts or other ingredients for coating into 6 equal rounds, each about as wide as an apple, on the waxed paper, spacing them well apart.

3. Pour water into the bottom pan of the double boiler to a depth of 1 to 2 inches. Set the pan on your stove and turn the heat on to high. Bring the water to a boil, about 5 minutes.

4. Put the caramels and the 2 tablespoons water in the top pan of the double boiler. Put the top pan of the double boiler over the bottom pan. Being very careful, heat the caramels, stirring often with the wooden spoon, until the caramels melt and are smooth, about 10 minutes.

5. Using pot holders, carefully lift out the top pan of the double boiler and set it on the hot pad. Holding an apple by the wooden stick, dip it in the hot caramel. Turn the apple to coat it evenly, using the spoon as needed to reach every surface. Lift the apple from the caramel, hold it over the pan, and twirl gently so that the excess caramel drips back into the pan. When the dripping stops, set the bottom of the apple on a round of nuts (or other coating) on the baking sheet. Tip and turn the apple so the nuts coat the sides. Repeat with the remaining apples. If the caramel gets too firm before you have coated all of the apples, return the top pan to the double boiler, turn on the heat to medium, and reheat the caramel until it is soft enough to coat. Put the tray of apples in a refrigerator until the caramel is set, at least 1 hour.

NUTRITIONAL ANALYSIS PER APPLE: Calories 434 (Kilojoules 1,823); Protein 5 g; Carbohydrates 70 g; Total Fat 18 g; Saturated Fat 5 g; Cholesterol 5 mg; Sodium 162 mg; Dietary Fiber 4 g

Pumpkin Bread

COOKING TIME: 40 MINUTES

INGREDIENTS

vegetable oil for greasing bread pans

2 cups all-purpose flour

1 teaspoon baking soda

¾ teaspoon ground cinnamon

¾ teaspoon ground nutmeg

½ teaspoon salt

¼ teaspoon ground ginger

1 cup granulated sugar

½ cup firmly packed dark brown sugar

1 cup canned pumpkin purée

½ cup vegetable oil

2 eggs

¼ cup water

EQUIPMENT

measuring cups and spoons

paper towel

four 5½-by-2½-inch loaf pans

medium mixing bowl

wooden spoon

large mixing bowl

electric mixer

rubber spatula

toothpick or table knife

cooling racks

pot holders

small, sharp knife, if needed

These wonderful mini sweet breads can be served for breakfast on Thanksgiving morning, with Thanksgiving dinner, or for a snack while you're waiting for the turkey to finish cooking. Pass softened or whipped cream cheese at the table for those who want to spread a little on the bread slices.

MAKES 4 MINI LOAVES

1. Adjust an oven rack to be in the center of your oven without another rack above it. Turn the oven on to 350°F. Pour oil onto the paper towel and evenly rub over the sides and bottom of the four 5½-by-2½-inch loaf pans. Set the pans aside.

2. Put the flour, baking soda, cinnamon, nutmeg, salt, and ginger in the medium mixing bowl. Stir with the wooden spoon until mixed. Set the bowl aside.

3. Put the granulated sugar, brown sugar, pumpkin, vegetable oil, and eggs in the large mixing bowl. With the electric mixer set on medium speed, beat until smooth and well blended. Turn off the mixer and scrape the sides of the bowl with the rubber spatula. Add the flour mixture, turn the mixer on low speed, and beat just until blended. Turn off the mixer and scrape the sides of the bowl with the spatula. Add the water and beat until blended. Spoon the batter into the prepared pans.

4. Place the pans in the preheated oven. Bake until the breads have risen and are cooked through, 35 to 40 minutes. To test if the bread is done, insert the toothpick or knife in the center of a bread. It should come out clean (without uncooked batter on it).

5. Put the cooling racks on your counter. Using pot holders, remove the pans from the oven and put them on the racks. Let cool for 10 minutes, then remove the breads from the pans and let cool completely on the racks. You should be able to turn a loaf pan upside down and the bread will fall out. If necessary, cut around the bread with the sharp knife to release it from the pan, and then turn the pan upside down. Slice and serve.

NUTRITIONAL ANALYSIS PER LOAF: Calories 847 (Kilojoules 3,557); Protein 10 g; Carbohydrates 130 g; Total Fat 33 g; Saturated Fat 5 g; Cholesterol 106 mg; Sodium 652 mg; Dietary Fiber 3 g

Baked Acorn Squash with Maple Cream

COOKING TIME: 1 HOUR

INGREDIENTS

2 small acorn squashes

4 teaspoons unsalted butter

salt and ground pepper to taste

4 tablespoons maple syrup

4 tablespoons heavy cream

EQUIPMENT

measuring spoons

cutting board

large, sharp knife

table spoon

baking dish

small saucepan

pastry brush

table fork

hot pad

pot holders

metal spatula

serving platter

Although this recipe produces a wonderfully sweet dish, it still counts as a vegetable on the Thanksgiving table. So if you are a dessert-loving kid, this is the recipe for you.

SERVES 4

1. Adjust an oven rack to be in the center of your oven without another rack above it. Turn the oven on to 350°F.

2. Put the squashes on the cutting board. With the large, sharp knife, cut each squash in half lengthwise. (Squash is a little hard to cut. You should ask an adult for help.)

3. With the spoon, scoop out and throw away the seeds and stringy fibers from the center of each squash half. With the knife, cut a thin slice from the bottom (skin side) of each squash half, so that each half sits flat in the baking dish. (Don't cut too much. You don't want to make a hole in the squash bowl. You could ask an adult for help here, too.)

4. Put the squash halves, hollow sides up, in a baking dish that will hold them without crowding.

5. Put the butter in the small saucepan. Set the pan on your stove and turn the heat on to low. Heat only until the butter melts. Put 1 teaspoon of the melted butter in the center of each squash half. With the pastry brush, brush the butter over the cut surface of each squash half.

6. Sprinkle the squash with salt and pepper. Put 1 tablespoon maple syrup into the center of each squash half. Add 1 tablespoon cream to the maple syrup in each squash half. Using the spoon, very lightly stir together the syrup and cream. They don't have to be well blended.

7. Put the baking dish on the center rack in the preheated oven. Bake until the squash is fork tender, about 1 hour. To test, insert the fork into the thickest part of a squash half; it should slide in easily.

8. Put the hot pad on your counter. Using pot holders, carefully remove the dish from the oven and put it on the hot pad. With the spatula, transfer the squash to the serving platter. Serve immediately.

NUTRITIONAL ANALYSIS PER SERVING: Calories 206 (Kilojoules 865); Protein 2 g; Carbohydrates 32 g; Total Fat 10 g; Saturated Fat 6 g; Cholesterol 31 mg; Sodium 13 mg; Dietary Fiber 6 g

Cranberry Sauce with Apple and Orange

COOKING TIME: 10 MINUTES

INGREDIENTS

about 4 cups fresh cranberries

2 oranges

1 apple

1 cup granulated sugar

EQUIPMENT

measuring cups

medium saucepan

box grater-shredder

cutting board

small, sharp knife

citrus juicer

long-handled wooden spoon

hot pad

pot holders

serving dish

plastic wrap

PREP TIP: Zest is the colored part of the citrus skin; the white part underneath is the pith and it is bitter. So when grating orange zest, be careful to remove only the orange part.

Cranberries are in season in November, which has made serving cranberry sauce along with roast turkey a Thanksgiving tradition. This recipe includes apples and oranges, too.

MAKES ABOUT 3 CUPS

1. Pick off any stems from the cranberries and throw them away. Throw away any mashed cranberries, too. Put the remaining cranberries in the medium saucepan. Set the saucepan aside.

2. Rub 1 orange over the small holes of the grater-shredder to remove the zest. Put the grated zest in the saucepan with the cranberries.

3. Put both oranges on the cutting board. With the small, sharp knife, cut the oranges in half crosswise. Using the citrus juicer, squeeze the juice from each orange half. Remove any seeds. Put the juice in a measuring cup. If necessary, add enough water to the juice to make 1 cup liquid. Pour into the saucepan with the cranberries.

4. Put the apple, stem end up, on the cutting board. With the knife, cut the apple into quarters. Cut away the stem and the core from the apple quarters (throw the stem and core away). Chop the apple into small pieces. Put the chopped apple and the sugar in the saucepan with the cranberries and juice.

5. Set the pan on your stove and turn the heat on to medium-high. Stirring constantly with the long-handled wooden spoon, bring the mixture to a boil. Stir and boil until all the cranberries pop open and the sauce has thickened, 5 to 10 minutes.

6. Put the hot pad on your counter. Using the pot holders, set the saucepan on the hot pad and let the sauce cool completely.

7. Transfer the cooled sauce to the serving dish. Cover the dish with plastic wrap. Refrigerate until ready to serve. Serve the sauce well chilled.

NUTRITIONAL ANALYSIS PER ¼-CUP SERVING: Calories 96 (Kilojoules 403); Protein 0 g; Carbohydrates 26 g; Total Fat 0 g; Saturated Fat 0 g; Cholesterol 0 mg; Sodium 1 mg; Dietary Fiber 2 g

Favorite Pumpkin Pie

COOKING TIME: 1 HOUR

INGREDIENTS

1 recipe Basic Pie Pastry (page 16)

2 eggs

1¾ cups pumpkin purée (15-ounce can)

1½ cups half-and-half

¾ cup granulated sugar

1 teaspoon ground cinnamon

¾ teaspoon ground allspice

¼ teaspoon salt

1 recipe Sweetened Whipped Cream (page 18)

EQUIPMENT

measuring cups and spoons

rolling pin

9-inch pie dish, 2 inches deep

table knife

medium mixing bowl

table fork

cooling rack

pot holders

plastic wrap

PREP TIP: Working with pie pastry dough can be tricky. Turn to page 16 to see two helpful photos.

Some history books say that pumpkin pie was served at the very first Thanksgiving feast. Native Americans did eat pumpkins and the English settlers were pie bakers, so it could be true.

SERVES 8

1. Prepare the pie pastry dough and chill as directed. Adjust an oven rack to be in the center of your oven without another rack above it. Turn the oven on to 425°F.

2. Roll out the dough into a circle ⅛ to ¼ inch thick. Carefully drape the dough around the rolling pin. Holding the rolling pin over the pie dish, carefully unwrap the dough, letting it fall gently onto the dish. Then ease the dough into the bottom and sides with your fingertips.

3. With the knife, trim the excess dough from around the edge of the pie dish, leaving a 1-inch overhang. With your fingers, crimp (pinch) the edge of the dough to make a pretty pattern around the edge of the pie dish. Set the pie shell aside.

4. Break the eggs into the medium bowl. With the fork, beat the eggs until blended. Add the pumpkin, half-and-half, sugar, cinnamon, all-spice, and salt to the eggs. Stir with the fork until the ingredients are very well blended. Carefully pour into the pie shell.

5. Put the pie dish on the center rack in the preheated oven. Bake the pie for 15 minutes. Turn down the oven temperature to 350°F. Continue baking until the pie is set and the pastry is a rich golden brown, 40 to 50 minutes longer. The pie is set when you can insert the knife into the center and the knife comes out clean (without uncooked filling on it).

6. Put the cooling rack on your counter. Turn off the oven. Using pot holders, remove the pie from the oven and set it on the cooling rack. Let the pie cool completely. Meanwhile, make the whipped cream, cover with plastic wrap, and refrigerate until serving.

7. Serve the pie with the whipped cream.

NUTRITIONAL ANALYSIS PER SERVING: Calories 345 (Kilojoules 1,449); Protein 5 g; Carbohydrates 42 g; Total Fat 18 g; Saturated Fat 7 g; Cholesterol 70 mg; Sodium 254 mg; Dietary Fiber 1 g

Great Turkey Melt

COOKING TIME: 5 MINUTES

INGREDIENTS

1 slice whole-wheat or coarse
country bread

2 teaspoons mayonnaise

about ¼ cup alfalfa sprouts

1 tomato

1 small red onion

1 large or several small slices
cooked turkey

2 thin slices Muenster or Monterey
jack cheese, cut the same size as
the bread

EQUIPMENT

measuring cups and spoons

toaster

table knife

baking sheet

cutting board

paring knife

serrated knife

plastic wrap

hot pad

pot holders

wide spatula

serving plate

One of the best things about Thanksgiving is having leftover turkey. Here is a special sandwich for the day after the feast. Other kinds of bread will work, too, including white bread, egg bread, French bread, a bagel half, or an English muffin half. Use a knife and fork to eat the sandwich.

SERVES 1

1. Toast the bread very lightly. Let the bread cool.

2. Adjust a broiler rack so that the top of the melt will be about 4 inches from the source of the heat. Turn the broiler on to high.

3. Using the table knife, spread the mayonnaise over one side of the toasted bread. Put the bread on the baking sheet with the mayonnaise-coated side up.

4. Cover the bread with a thin layer of the alfalfa sprouts.

5. Put the tomato on the cutting board. With the paring knife, cut out the stem end. Steady the tomato and, with the serrated knife, cut 2 slices from it. Arrange the tomato slices on top of the alfalfa sprouts. Wrap the rest of the tomato in plastic wrap and refrigerate for another use.

6. Steady the onion on the cutting board. With the paring knife, cut off the stem end and throw it away. Cut 2 very thin slices from the onion. Pull off the papery skin from each onion slice. Arrange the onion slices on top of the tomato slices. Wrap the rest of the onion in plastic wrap and refrigerate for another use.

7. Arrange the turkey in an even layer over the onion slices. Lay the cheese slices over the turkey.

8. Put the baking sheet under the broiler and broil the sandwich until the cheese melts and starts to turn light golden brown, about 5 minutes.

9. Put the hot pad on your counter. Using pot holders, remove the baking sheet from the broiler and set on the hot pad. With the spatula, transfer the sandwich to the serving plate. Serve immediately.

NUTRITIONAL ANALYSIS PER SERVING: Calories 420 (Kilojoules 1,764); Protein 36 g; Carbohydrates 22 g; Total Fat 21 g; Saturated Fat 8 g; Cholesterol 98 mg; Sodium 454 mg; Dietary Fiber 4 g

Best Roast Chicken

COOKING TIME: 1½ HOURS

INGREDIENTS

1 tablespoon olive oil

about 2 teaspoons Dijon mustard

salt and ground pepper to taste

1 chicken, 3½ to 4 pounds

6 fresh tarragon, thyme, or oregano sprigs

fresh herb sprigs for garnish (optional)

EQUIPMENT

measuring spoons

roasting rack

shallow roasting pan

scissors

kitchen string

ruler

small mixing bowl

table fork

paper towels

pastry brush

instant-read thermometer or small, sharp knife

hot pad

pot holders

carving fork or metal tongs

serving platter

Roast chicken is an excellent choice for Hanukkah dinner. Ask an adult to help with transferring the chicken to the platter and with carving. Garnish with small halved apples, if you like.

SERVES 4 TO 6

1. Arrange a rack to be in the center of your oven without another rack above it. Turn on the oven to 350°F. Put the roasting rack in the roasting pan. With the scissors, cut a piece of string about 6 inches long.

2. Put the olive oil, mustard, salt, and pepper in the small bowl. Beat with the fork until well combined. Set aside.

3. Remove the giblets (heart, liver, gizzard) and any fat from the chicken's body cavity and set them aside. Rinse the chicken inside and outside under cold running water and dry well with paper towels.

4. With the pastry brush, brush a little of the oil mixture over the inside of the chicken. Place the giblets and 2 of the herb sprigs in the cavity. Put the chicken breast side up. With the string, tie the ends of the drumsticks together. Tuck the wing tips under the chicken. Place the chicken, breast side up, on the rack. Brush the remaining oil mixture over the outside. Place the remaining 4 herb sprigs on top of the chicken. If you have it, place a piece of fat (about the size of a quarter) from the cavity of the chicken on top of the herb sprigs.

5. Set the roasting pan on the center rack in the preheated oven. Roast the chicken, uncovered, until it is deep golden brown and cooked through, 1¼ to 1½ hours. You can tell if the chicken is cooked by one of two methods: Insert an instant-read thermometer into the thickest part of the thigh (not touching the bone); it should read 180°F. Or, using the sharp knife, pierce the joint between the thigh and the leg; if the juices that run out are clear instead of pink, the chicken is cooked. (Ask an adult to help.)

6. Put the hot pad on your counter. Using pot holders, transfer the pan to the hot pad. Let the chicken rest for 10 minutes before serving.

7. To serve, snip the string on the chicken and discard it. If the piece of fat is still on the chicken, throw it away. With the carving fork or tongs, transfer the chicken to the platter. Garnish with fresh herbs, if you like.

NUTRITIONAL ANALYSIS PER SERVING: Calories 377 (Kilojoules 1,583); Protein 41 g; Carbohydrates 0 g; Total Fat 22 g; Saturated Fat 6 g; Cholesterol 132 mg; Sodium 171 mg; Dietary Fiber 0 g

Potato Latkes

COOKING TIME: 20 MINUTES

INGREDIENTS

1 egg

2 medium baking potatoes

1 very small yellow onion

¼ teaspoon salt

big pinch of pepper

pinch of ground nutmeg

3 tablespoons all-purpose flour

vegetable oil for cooking

applesauce or sour cream for
   serving (optional)

EQUIPMENT

measuring cups and spoons

electric blender

cutting board

vegetable peeler

small, sharp knife

rubber spatula

paper towels

large plate

large, heavy frying pan

metal spatula

Although these potato pancakes are traditionally served during Hanukkah, they are a crowd pleaser any time of the year. Applesauce and sour cream are favorite toppings.

SERVES 4

1. Break the egg into the container of the electric blender; set aside.

2. Put the potatoes on the cutting board and peel them with the vegetable peeler. With the small, sharp knife, cut the potatoes into bite-sized pieces. Put the pieces in the blender container with the egg.

3. Put the onion on the cutting board. With the knife, cut the onion in half from the root to the stem end. Place each onion half, flat side down, on the cutting board and cut off a thin slice from the root and stem ends. Cut each onion half in half again. Pull off all the papery skin (throw the skin away). Add the onion to the blender along with the salt, pepper, nutmeg, and flour.

4. Put the lid on the blender. Turn the blender on and blend just until the potatoes and onions are coarsely chopped and the ingredients are mixed. Do not blend to a liquid. To make sure the ingredients are evenly chopped, turn the blender off a few times and scrape the sides with the rubber spatula.

5. Put a few paper towels on the large plate; set the plate on your kitchen counter near your stove. Pour enough oil into the large, heavy frying pan to form a thin layer. Set the pan on your stove and turn the heat on to medium-high. Heat the oil until it is hot. To make each pancake, gently drop about ¼ cup of the potato mixture into the frying pan. Make only a few pancakes at a time and do not crowd the pan. With the metal spatula, lightly flatten the top of each pancake. Fry until golden brown on the underside, 2 to 3 minutes. With the spatula, turn each pancake over and fry until brown on the second side, 2 to 3 minutes longer. (The first batch might be hard to turn over, but the second batch will be easier.) With the spatula, carefully transfer the pancakes to the paper towels. Keep warm. Continue making the pancakes until all the batter has been used.

6. Serve the hot pancakes with applesauce or sour cream, if you like.

NUTRITIONAL ANALYSIS PER SERVING: Calories 194 (Kilojoules 815); Protein 4 g; Carbohydrates 22 g; Total Fat 10 g; Saturated Fat 2 g; Cholesterol 54 mg; Sodium 164 mg; Dietary Fiber 2 g

Golden Gelt

COOKING TIME: 10 MINUTES,
    PLUS 30 MINUTES FOR
    CHILLING

INGREDIENTS

½ cup water

¼ cup granulated sugar

4 large navel oranges

EQUIPMENT

measuring cups

small saucepan

long-handled wooden spoon

hot pad

pot holders

cutting board

small, sharp knife

serving bowl

plastic wrap

SAFETY TIP: Ask an adult for help when it comes time to heat the water and sugar.

During Hanukkah, grown-ups often give kids little round chocolate candies wrapped in gold foil. The candy is called gelt because it looks like money, and gelt is the Yiddish word for money. You can turn the tables by wishing grown-ups a happy Hanukkah with this dish of sweet oranges. Here, the oranges are called gelt because they are coin shaped and gold, and you can bank on them to be delicious.

SERVES 4

1. Put the water and sugar in the small saucepan. Set the pan on your stove, turn the heat on to medium, and bring the mixture to a boil, stirring constantly with the long-handled wooden spoon. When the sugar is completely dissolved (you won't be able to see any grains) and the mixture is boiling, turn the heat to low so that the mixture simmers. Without stirring, simmer the mixture for 3 minutes.

2. Put the hot pad on your counter. Using pot holders, remove the pan from the burner and put it on the hot pad. Let the syrup cool completely.

3. Put 1 orange on the cutting board. With the small, sharp knife, cut a thin slice off each end to expose the fruit. Stand the orange upright and slice off the peel in strips, cutting around the contour of the orange to expose the fruit. Do not leave any of the white membrane on the fruit (it is very bitter). Remove the peels from the remaining oranges in the same way. Cut the oranges crosswise into rounds.

4. Arrange the orange rounds in a pretty serving bowl. Pour the cooled syrup over the oranges. Cover the bowl with plastic wrap and refrigerate just until chilled, about 30 minutes. Serve chilled.

NUTRITIONAL ANALYSIS PER SERVING: Calories 127 (Kilojoules 533); Protein 2 g; Carbohydrates 32 g; Total Fat 0 g; Saturated Fat 0 g; Cholesterol 0 mg; Sodium 2 mg; Dietary Fiber 4 g

Christmas Morning French Toast

COOKING TIME: 20 MINUTES

INGREDIENTS

vegetable oil for baking sheet

3 eggs

1 cup eggnog

2 teaspoons granulated sugar

½ teaspoon vanilla extract

⅛ teaspoon ground nutmeg

pinch of salt

8 slices white or whole-wheat bread

¼ cup unsalted butter, plus 2 tablespoons for serving (optional)

½ cup maple syrup for serving

EQUIPMENT

measuring cups and spoons

pastry brush

baking sheet

medium shallow mixing bowl

table fork

aluminum foil

8 pieces waxed paper cut into
4-inch squares

small saucepan

hot pad

pot holders

metal spatula

plates for serving

This dish is made up to one week before Christmas and then put in the freezer. Just pop it into an oven on Christmas morning and enjoy.

SERVES 4

1. Brush the baking sheet with oil and set it aside.

2. Break the eggs into the shallow bowl. Using the fork, beat the eggs until the yolks and whites are well blended. Add the eggnog, sugar, vanilla, nutmeg, and salt. Beat with the fork until well blended.

3. Dip 1 slice of the bread in the egg mixture and let it soak for about 1 minute. With the fork, turn the bread over and let the second side soak until saturated. Put the egg-soaked bread on the oiled baking sheet. Repeat with the remaining bread. Cover the baking sheet with aluminum foil and put it in the freezer until the bread is completely frozen. Stack the frozen slices together, slipping a square of waxed paper between them. Wrap the stack in foil and freeze for up to 1 week.

4. To bake, adjust an oven rack to be in the center of your oven without another rack above it. Turn the oven on to 425°F. Put the butter in the small saucepan. Set the pan on your stove, turn the heat on to low, and melt the ¼ cup butter.

5. Remove the bread from the freezer. Unwrap the bread and remove the waxed paper. With the pastry brush, brush one side of each piece of bread with melted butter. Place the bread, buttered side down, in a single layer on the ungreased baking sheet. Place the baking sheet in the preheated oven. Bake the French toast for 10 minutes.

6. Put the hot pad on your counter. Using pot holders, remove the baking sheet from the oven and put it on the hot pad. Brush the remaining butter evenly over the tops of the toast slices. Turn the toast over with the spatula so the buttered side is down. Return the baking sheet to the oven and continue to bake until the toast is golden brown, 5 to 10 minutes.

7. Using pot holders, remove the baking sheet from the oven and put it on the hot pad. With the spatula, transfer the French toast to the plates. Serve with the 2 tablespoons butter and the syrup on the side.

NUTRITIONAL ANALYSIS PER SERVING: Calories 507 (Kilojoules 2,129); Protein 11 g; Carbohydrates 62 g; Total Fat 24 g; Saturated Fat 13 g; Cholesterol 234 mg; Sodium 410 mg; Dietary Fiber 1 g

Crisp Vegetable Wreath with Herb-Yogurt Dip

INGREDIENTS

FOR THE DIP

6 green onions

2 fresh dill sprigs

1 cup plain yogurt

1 cup cottage cheese

¼ cup loosely packed fresh parsley leaves

about ½ teaspoon celery salt

about 2 drops hot-pepper sauce (optional)

1 small head cauliflower

1 medium stalk broccoli

about 16 cherry tomatoes

fresh herb sprigs for garnish (optional)

EQUIPMENT

measuring cups and spoons

cutting board

small, sharp knife

electric blender

rubber spatula

container with a cover

plastic bags

table spoon

small, shallow bowl

large plate or tray

This wreath of red, green, and white vegetables makes a healthful and festive addition to the holiday table. Sugar snap peas, snow peas, cucumbers, celery, green beans, red bell peppers, radishes, and jicama can be substituted for the vegetables listed here.

SERVES 8

1. First, make the dip: Put the green onions on the cutting board. With the small, sharp knife, cut off the roots of each onion and peel off the outer layer of skin. Cut off the dark leaves about 3 inches above the white root end. Put the pieces of white and pale green leaves in the blender. Put the dill on the cutting board. With the knife, chop enough dill leaves to fill 1 tablespoon. Add the chopped dill, yogurt, cottage cheese, parsley, ½ teaspoon celery salt, and 2 drops hot-pepper sauce, if using, to the blender. Put the lid securely on the blender. Turn the blender on high speed and blend until the ingredients are smooth and creamy. To blend properly, you may have to turn off the blender several times and rearrange the ingredients with the rubber spatula. Taste the dip. Add more celery salt and pepper sauce to make it taste good to you. Put the lid on the blender and again blend until well combined. Put the dip in the covered container and refrigerate until you are ready to serve.

2. Now, prepare the vegetables: Using your fingers, pull off all of the green leaves from around the cauliflower head. Put the cauliflower, rounded side down, on the cutting board. With the small, sharp knife, cut the white core from the center of the cauliflower stem end. With your fingers, break the cauliflower into individual florets. Put the large florets on the cutting board and cut in half to make dipping-sized pieces. Put the broccoli on the cutting board. With the knife, cut off the tough, thick broccoli stem. Cut the broccoli into dipping-sized florets.

3. With your fingers, remove any stems from the cherry tomatoes. If you are not serving the dip and vegetables immediately, put the vegetables in plastic bags and keep in the crisper in your refrigerator.

4. To serve, spoon the dip into the small, shallow bowl. Put the bowl in the center of the large plate or tray. Surround the bowl with the vegetables, arranging them to resemble a Christmas wreath. Garnish with fresh herbs, if you like, and serve immediately.

NUTRITIONAL ANALYSIS PER SERVING: Calories 64 (Kilojoules 269); Protein 6 g; Carbohydrates 6 g; Total Fat 2 g; Saturated Fat 1 g; Cholesterol 8 mg; Sodium 172 mg; Dietary Fiber 2 g

Mashed Sweet Potatoes with Brown Sugar and Pecans

COOKING TIME: 35 MINUTES

INGREDIENTS

6 sweet potatoes

¼ cup unsalted butter

2½ tablespoons brown sugar

½ teaspoon salt

2 tablespoons chopped pecans

EQUIPMENT

measuring cups and spoons

cutting board

vegetable peeler

small, sharp knife

large saucepan

table fork

small saucepan

colander

6-cup baking dish

pastry brush

large mixing bowl

potato masher

mixing spoon

hot pad

pot holders

SAFETY TIP: Handling a pot of boiling water is dangerous. Ask an adult for help when it comes time to drain the sweet potatoes.

There are two popular kinds of sweet potatoes: one is gold and the other is orange and sometimes called a "yam." You can use either for this dish. It's a perfect addition to the Christmas menu.

SERVES 6

1. Put 1 sweet potato on the cutting board. Peel with the vegetable peeler. With the small, sharp knife, trim off the ends. Cut out any small brown spots in the potato. Peel and trim the remaining 5 potatoes.

2. Put the peeled potatoes in the large saucepan. Add enough cold water to cover the potatoes by 1 inch. Set the pan on your stove, turn the heat on to medium-high, and bring the water to a boil. Reduce the heat slightly and gently boil the potatoes until tender, 20 to 25 minutes. To test, insert the fork into the thickest part of a potato; it should glide in easily.

3. Put the butter in the small saucepan. Set the pan on your stove, turn the heat on to low, and melt the butter. Turn off the heat and let the butter sit while you continue with the recipe.

4. Put the colander in your sink. Ask an adult to pour the cooked sweet potatoes into the colander.

5. Adjust an oven rack to be in the center of your oven without another rack above it. Turn the oven on to 350°F. Put 1 tablespoon of the melted butter in the 6-cup baking dish. With the pastry brush, brush some of the melted butter over the sides and bottom of the dish.

6. Put the potatoes in the large mixing bowl. Mash the potatoes with the potato masher until they are smooth. Stir in 2 tablespoons of the melted butter, 1 tablespoon of the brown sugar, and the salt until well mixed. Spoon the mashed potato mixture into the baking dish. Sprinkle the remaining butter, the remaining 1½ tablespoons brown sugar, and the chopped pecans evenly over the top.

7. Place the baking dish on the center rack in the preheated oven. Bake until the sugar melts and the mixture is piping hot, about 15 minutes.

8. Place the hot pad on the dining table. Using pot holders, transfer the baking dish to the hot pad. Serve immediately.

NUTRITIONAL ANALYSIS PER SERVING: Calories 276 (Kilojoules 1,159); Protein 3 g; Carbohydrates 46 g; Total Fat 10 g; Saturated Fat 5 g; Cholesterol 21 mg; Sodium 218 mg; Dietary Fiber 5 g

Festive Winter Salad

COOKING TIME: 10 MINUTES

INGREDIENTS

8 cups mixed torn salad greens (about ½ pound)

3 ounces fresh goat cheese

1 tablespoon red wine vinegar

3 tablespoons olive oil

½ teaspoon Dijon mustard

¼ to ½ teaspoon salt

⅛ teaspoon pepper

3 ripe pears

3 tablespoons unsalted butter

1½ tablespoons granulated sugar

½ cup pecan halves

EQUIPMENT

measuring cups and spoons

colander

paper towels or salad spinner

large salad bowl

plastic wrap

small bowl

table fork

vegetable peeler

cutting board

small, sharp knife

large nonstick frying pan

metal spatula

hot pad

pot holders

2 large spoons

This is a very sophisticated salad to serve at special wintertime feasts. Mixed salad greens are available at many markets. If you want to create your own mix, use a variety of greens, such as romaine, butter, and leaf lettuces and radicchio. Separate the leaves and tear them into big pieces.

SERVES 6

1. Put the greens in the colander and rinse with cold running water. Drain well. Gently pat the greens very dry with paper towels or spin them in the salad spinner. Put the greens in the salad bowl.

2. With your fingers, coarsely crumble the goat cheese and sprinkle the crumbles over the greens. Cover the salad bowl with plastic wrap and refrigerate until ready to serve.

3. Just before serving, make the dressing: Put the vinegar, olive oil, mustard, salt, and pepper in the small bowl. Beat with the fork until the ingredients are blended. Set the dressing aside.

4. With the vegetable peeler, peel each pear (see page 15). Put the pears on the cutting board. With the small, sharp knife, quarter each pear lengthwise. Cut away the stem and core from the pear quarters. Cut each pear quarter lengthwise in half (you should have 24 wedges).

5. Put the butter in the large nonstick frying pan. Set the pan on your stove, turn the heat on to medium, and melt the butter. Add the pear wedges and sauté for 1 minute, gently turning the pears with the spatula to coat the pears with butter. Sprinkle the sugar over the pears. Continue cooking the pears, turning occasionally, until the sugar and butter blend and the mixture is syrupy, about 2 minutes. Add the pecans to the frying pan and continue cooking and turning until the pears are well glazed and begin to brown and the pecans are glazed and heated through, about 3 minutes. Put the hot pad on your counter. Using pot holders, set the frying pan on the hot pad.

6. Remove the greens from the refrigerator. Stir the dressing with the fork and pour over the greens. Toss gently with the large spoons. Spoon on the pear mixture and toss again. Serve immediately.

NUTRITIONAL ANALYSIS PER SERVING: Calories 281 (Kilojoules 1,180); Protein 4 g; Carbohydrates 19 g; Total Fat 22 g; Saturated Fat 7 g; Cholesterol 22 mg; Sodium 218 mg; Dietary Fiber 3 g

Corn Kernel Spoon Bread

COOKING TIME: 45 MINUTES

INGREDIENTS

softened unsalted butter for
  greasing baking dish

4 eggs

1 cup milk

2 cups water

2 tablespoons unsalted butter

1½ teaspoons salt

1 cup white cornmeal

1 cup frozen corn kernels, thawed

EQUIPMENT

measuring cups and spoons

2-quart round baking dish

medium mixing bowl

table fork

large saucepan

long-handled wooden spoon

hot pad

pot holders

Spoon bread, a specialty of southern cooks, is crusty and golden brown on the outside and soft and creamy in the center. It is a cross between corn bread and a soufflé. Spoon bread should be whisked straight to the holiday table from the oven and spooned onto plates while steaming hot. Add a pat of butter on top, if you like.

SERVES 6 TO 8

1. Adjust an oven rack to be in the center of your oven without another rack above it. Turn the oven on to 425°F. Evenly butter the baking dish and set the dish aside.

2. Break the eggs into the medium bowl. Add the milk. With the table fork, beat the eggs and milk until they are well blended; set the mixture aside.

3. Put the water, butter, and salt in the large saucepan. Set the pan on your stove, turn the heat on to high, and bring the mixture to a rapid boil. Stirring constantly with the long-handled wooden spoon, very slowly stir the cornmeal into the boiling water. Reduce the heat to medium. Stirring constantly, cook the mixture until it becomes thick, about 1 minute. Turn off the heat.

4. Put the hot pad on your counter. Using pot holders, set the pan on the hot pad. Add the egg-milk mixture to the cornmeal mixture and stir with the spoon until the ingredients are well combined. Stir in the corn kernels.

5. Pour the mixture into the buttered baking dish. Put the baking dish in the preheated oven. Bake, uncovered, until the spoon bread is set, puffy, and golden brown, about 40 minutes.

6. Turn off the oven. Place the hot pad on the dining table. Using pot holders, remove the baking dish from the oven and set it on the hot pad. Serve immediately.

NUTRITIONAL ANALYSIS PER SERVING: Calories 190 (Kilojoules 798); Protein 7 g; Carbohydrates 22 g; Total Fat 8 g; Saturated Fat 4 g; Cholesterol 137 mg; Sodium 553 mg; Dietary Fiber 0 g

Popovers

COOKING TIME: 40 MINUTES

INGREDIENTS

softened unsalted butter for
  buttering custard cups

2 eggs

1 cup milk

½ teaspoon salt

1 cup all-purpose flour

2 tablespoons unsalted butter

EQUIPMENT

measuring cups and spoons

six ¾-cup custard cups or popover
  pan

medium mixing bowl

table fork

small saucepan

baking sheet

hot pad

pot holders

kitchen towel

serving plates

table knife, if needed

Eating a popover is like eating air wrapped in a thin layer of dough. Make popovers to accompany a holiday dinner or to have for breakfast with butter and jam. You can make popovers in custard cups or a popover pan.

MAKES 6 POPOVERS

1. Adjust an oven rack to be in the center of your oven without another rack above it. Turn the oven on to 425°F. Generously grease the custard cups or popover pan cups with butter. Set the cups aside.

2. Put the eggs, milk, and salt in the medium bowl. Beat with the fork until the mixture is well blended. Add the flour and beat with the fork just until the mixture is smooth and blended.

3. Put the butter in the small saucepan. Set the pan on your stove, turn the heat on to low, and melt the butter.

4. Spoon 1 teaspoon of the melted butter into the bottom of each cup. Pour the batter into the cups, dividing it evenly among them.

5. If using custard cups, place them on the baking sheet (for easy handling). Put the baking sheet or popover pan on the center rack in the preheated oven. Bake until the popovers appear firm on the outside, are high above the rim of the cups, and are deep golden brown, 30 to 40 minutes.

6. Put the hot pad on your counter. Using pot holders, remove the baking sheet or popover pan from the oven and put it on the hot pad. Being careful not to burn yourself, and using the kitchen towel to protect your fingers, tip the popovers out of the cups and put them on the serving plates. (If necessary, loosen the popovers with the tip of the table knife, and then turn them out of the cups.) Serve the popovers immediately.

NUTRITIONAL ANALYSIS PER POPOVER: Calories 176 (Kilojoules 739); Protein 6 g; Carbohydrates 18 g; Total Fat 9 g; Saturated Fat 5 g; Cholesterol 92 mg; Sodium 235 mg; Dietary Fiber 1 g

Old-Fashioned Gingerbread

COOKING TIME: 50 MINUTES,
PLUS 15 MINUTES FOR
COOLING

INGREDIENTS

unsalted butter for greasing cake pan

½ cup unsalted butter

2½ cups all-purpose flour

1½ teaspoons baking soda

1 teaspoon ground cinnamon

1 teaspoon ground ginger

pinch of salt

½ cup light molasses

½ cup honey

1 cup hot water

1 egg

½ cup granulated sugar

1 teaspoon vanilla extract

EQUIPMENT

measuring cups and spoons

9-inch square cake pan with 2-inch
sides

small saucepan

2 medium mixing bowls

mixing spoon

large mixing bowl

electric mixer

toothpick

cooling rack

pot holders

table knife

metal spatula

serving plate

Gingerbread is filled with sugar and spice and everything nice. It is perfect for serving at a casual holiday dinner or for a daytime open house. Top each serving with a dusting of confectioners' sugar, if you like. You can use a stencil to make a festive design.

SERVES 9

1. Grease the cake pan with butter. Set the pan aside. Arrange a rack to be in the center of your oven without another rack above it. Turn the oven on to 325°F.

2. Put the butter in the saucepan. Set the pan on your stove, turn the heat on to low, and melt the butter. Set the butter aside to cool slightly.

3. Put the flour, baking soda, cinnamon, ginger, and salt in a medium bowl. Stir with the spoon until the ingredients are well combined. Set the flour mixture aside.

4. Put the molasses, honey, and hot water in the other medium bowl. Stir with the spoon until well mixed. Set aside.

5. Put the melted butter, egg, sugar, and vanilla in the large mixing bowl. Using the electric mixer set on medium speed, beat until the ingredients are well combined. Add one-third of the flour mixture and beat until blended. Add one-half of the liquid mixture and beat on low speed until blended. Add one-half of the remaining flour mixture and beat just until blended. Add the remaining liquid mixture and beat until blended, then add the remaining flour mixture and beat just until it disappears.

6. Pour the batter into the greased cake pan. Set the pan on the center rack in the preheated oven and bake until the cake is set and the tooth-pick inserted into the center comes out clean, 45 to 50 minutes.

7. Put the cooling rack on your counter. Using pot holders, remove the pan from the oven and put it on the cooling rack. Let the cake cool for at least 15 minutes. Serve warm or let cool completely.

8. To serve, cut the gingerbread into 9 squares with the table knife. Remove the squares from the pan with the metal spatula and put them on the serving plate.

NUTRITIONAL ANALYSIS PER SERVING: Calories 380 (Kilojoules 1,596); Protein 4 g; Carbohydrates 66 g; Total Fat 12 g; Saturated Fat 7 g; Cholesterol 52 mg; Sodium 242 mg; Dietary Fiber 1 g

Holiday Cookies

COOKING TIME: 12 MINUTES

INGREDIENTS

1 recipe Basic Butter Cookie Dough (*page 17*)

solid vegetable shortening for greasing baking sheets

2 recipes Basic Icing (*page 18*)

food colorings

colored sugars for decorating

EQUIPMENT

2 baking sheets

holiday cookie cutters

metal spatula

rolling pin

cooling racks

hot pads

pot holders

small bowls, if tinting icing

spoons

icing spatula

rubber spatula

pastry bag with plain writing tip (optional)

PREP TIP: To make decorated cookies without icing, decorate the cookies with candies, nuts, sprinkles, or colored sugars after the cookies are cut and are on the baking sheets, but before baking the cookies (after step 2 but before step 3). Bake the cookies as directed and let cool completely.

These cookies are fun to make, pretty to see, and delicious to eat. You can make the cookies for Christmas, Hanukkah, or any other holiday, and you can decorate them in many different ways. Try using icy, wintry colors for the winter holidays.

MAKES ABOUT 40 COOKIES

1. Prepare the cookie dough and roll out as directed. Adjust 2 oven racks to be in the center of your oven. Turn the oven on to 350°F. Lightly grease the baking sheets with the vegetable shortening.

2. Using a cookie cutter, press it straight down into the dough to cut out a shape, then lift carefully. Repeat, cutting close to the first one, until you have cut out as many cookies as you can. Gently slip the metal spatula under the dough shapes and transfer to the baking sheets. Set the scraps aside. Roll out and cut the second piece of dough. Transfer to the baking sheets. Gather all the dough scraps together, then roll out, cut, and transfer to the baking sheets.

3. Place the baking sheets on the center racks in the preheated oven. Bake until the cookies are light golden brown around the edges, 10 to 12 minutes.

4. Put the cooling racks and hot pads on your counter. With pot holders, transfer the baking sheets to the hot pads. With the metal spatula, transfer the cookies to the racks. Let cool completely.

5. To make iced decorated cookies, prepare the Basic Icing. If you want to tint the icing different colors, divide it among small bowls. For icy, wintry colors, add 1 or 2 drops of different food coloring to each bowl. Stir each mixture with a spoon until the color is evenly distributed. With the icing spatula, spread a thin layer of icing over each cookie.

6. With the rubber spatula, put some icing in the pastry bag fitted with the writing tip and decorate the cookies with dots and stripes, if you like.

7. Decorate the cookies with the colored sugars. Set the cookies aside until the icing is completely dry, about 30 minutes.

NUTRITIONAL ANALYSIS PER COOKIE: Calories 122 (Kilojoules 512); Protein 1 g; Carbohydrates 20 g; Total Fat 5 g; Saturated Fat 3 g; Cholesterol 17 mg; Sodium 29 mg; Dietary Fiber 0 g

Carolers' Hot Chocolate

COOKING TIME: 15 MINUTES

INGREDIENTS

⅓ cup unsweetened cocoa powder

¼ cup granulated sugar

pinch of salt

3 cups milk

½ teaspoon vanilla extract

9 large marshmallows

EQUIPMENT

measuring cups and spoons

medium saucepan

long-handled wooden spoon

ladle

4 mugs or cups

At Christmastime, when carolers stop by, invite them in for a warming cup of this rich hot chocolate. Or you can make hot chocolate on a chilly afternoon to help keep you warm.

SERVES 4

1. Put the cocoa, sugar, and salt in the medium saucepan. Stir with the wooden spoon until the ingredients are well blended. Add a small amount of the milk and stir to make a smooth paste. Stir in the remaining milk.

2. Set the pan on your stove. Turn the heat on to medium and cook the mixture, stirring constantly, until tiny bubbles form around the edges of the pan (do not boil), about 8 minutes.

3. Turn the heat to low. Add the vanilla and 5 of the marshmallows to the saucepan. Cook, stirring constantly, until the marshmallows melt, about 5 minutes.

4. Ladle the hot chocolate into 4 mugs or cups. Add 1 marshmallow to each mug or cup and serve immediately.

NUTRITIONAL ANALYSIS PER SERVING: Calories 229 (Kilojoules 962); Protein 8 g; Carbohydrates 38 g; Total Fat 7 g; Saturated Fat 4 g; Cholesterol 26 mg; Sodium 134 mg; Dietary Fiber 2 g

New Year's Toasts

COOKING TIME: 10 MINUTES

INGREDIENTS

3 slices white or whole-wheat bread

FOR SWEET, CREAMY STRAWBERRY TOPPING

2 tablespoons cream cheese, softened

1 tablespoon strawberry jam

FOR SUGAR PECAN TOPPING

1 tablespoon unsalted butter, softened

1 tablespoon chopped pecans

1 teaspoon dark brown sugar

FOR ORANGE COCONUT TOPPING

1 small orange

2 teaspoons unsalted butter, softened

1 teaspoon honey

2 teaspoons shredded dried coconut

EQUIPMENT

measuring spoons

table knife

box grater-shredder

baking sheet

hot pad

pot holders

metal spatula

serving plates

New Year's Eve calls for good old-fashioned traditions like making noise to ring out the old year and making toasts to ring in the new. These kid-style New Year's toasts are a perfect way to celebrate.

SERVES 2

1. Adjust a rack to be in the center of your oven without another rack above it. Turn the oven on to 425°F.

2. Cut away the crust from the bread slices.

3. For the sweet, creamy strawberry toasts, use the table knife to spread the cream cheese on one side of 1 slice of bread. Then spread the strawberry jam evenly over the cream cheese. Cut the slice of bread in half on the diagonal to make 2 triangles.

4. For the sugar pecan toasts, use the table knife to spread the butter on one side of 1 slice of bread. Sprinkle the pecans and then the brown sugar evenly over the butter. Cut the slice of bread in half on the diagonal to make 2 triangles.

5. For the orange coconut toasts, rub the orange over the small holes of the grater to remove the zest. You will need ¼ teaspoon zest. (Reserve the orange for another use—or eat it now.) Use the table knife to spread the butter on one side of the remaining slice of bread. Then spread the honey evenly over the butter. Sprinkle the grated zest over the honey, then sprinkle with the coconut. Cut the slice of bread in half on the diagonal to make 2 triangles.

6. Put the bread, topping side up, on the ungreased baking sheet. Put the baking sheet in the preheated oven. Bake until the toasts are crisp, about 8 minutes.

7. Put the hot pad on your counter. Using pot holders, remove the baking sheet from the oven and put it on the hot pad. Using the metal spatula, transfer the toasts to the plates. Serve immediately.

NUTRITIONAL ANALYSIS PER SERVING: Calories 322 (Kilojoules 1,350); Protein 5 g; Carbohydrates 23 g; Total Fat 19 g; Saturated Fat 10 g; Cholesterol 42 mg; Sodium 254 mg; Dietary Fiber 2 g

Chocolate Fondue

COOKING TIME: 15 MINUTES

INGREDIENTS

2 pints strawberries

3 ripe bananas

3 apples

½ lemon

2 cups granulated sugar

1 can (13 ounces) evaporated milk

3 ounces unsweetened chocolate

pinch of ground cinnamon

1 teaspoon vanilla extract

half-and-half or milk for thinning
  fondue (optional)

EQUIPMENT

measuring cups and spoons

cutting board

small, sharp knife

heatproof serving bowl and serving
  platter

plastic wrap

medium saucepan

long-handled wooden spoon

hot pad

pot holders

electric mixer

fondue skewers or table forks

SAFETY TIP: Ask an adult for help
when it comes time to beat the
chocolate mixture.

Here's a sweet way to start the new year. Try any of your favorite fruits, fresh or dried, or chunks of pound or angelfood cake in place of the fruits suggested here. If you have a fondue pot, pour the chocolate mixture into it for serving.

SERVES 8

1. Put the strawberries on the cutting board. With the small, sharp knife, remove the green stems from the strawberries. Cut very large berries in half lengthwise.

2. Peel the bananas and put them on the cutting board. With the knife, cut them on the diagonal into slices 1 inch thick.

3. Put an apple, stem end up, on the cutting board. With the small, sharp knife, cut the apple into quarters. Cut away the core from the apple quarters. Repeat quartering and coring the remaining apples. Squeeze some lemon juice over the cut sides of the apples to keep them from turning brown.

4. Put the heatproof serving bowl in the center of the serving platter. Arrange the fruits in clusters around the bowl. Cover with plastic wrap and refrigerate until ready to serve.

5. Put the sugar, milk, chocolate, and cinnamon in the medium saucepan. Set the pan on your stove and turn the heat on to low. Cook, stirring constantly with the long-handled wooden spoon, until smooth, about 15 minutes. Do not let the mixture boil. Turn off the heat.

6. Put the hot pad on your counter. Using pot holders, remove the pan from the burner and put it on the hot pad. Add the vanilla to the chocolate mixture. With the electric mixer set on medium-high speed, beat the mixture until it is smooth and well blended, about 2 minutes. If you want the fondue to be a little thinner, beat in half-and-half or milk, 1 tablespoon at a time, until the consistency is just right.

7. With the help of an adult, pour the hot fondue into the heatproof serving bowl. Serve immediately with the fruit. To eat, spear a piece of fruit with a skewer or fork and dip into the warm fondue until the fruit is covered with chocolate.

NUTRITIONAL ANALYSIS PER SERVING: Calories 413 (Kilojoules 1,735); Protein 6 g; Carbohydrates 82 g; Total Fat 10 g; Saturated Fat 6 g; Cholesterol 15 mg; Sodium 57 mg; Dietary Fiber 6 g

GLOSSARY

This alphabetical list gives you simple explanations for cooking terms and ingredients that you will find in this book and other cookbooks. If you can't find what you are looking for, ask an adult for help.

A

ADJUST SEASONING
To taste food before serving and then add seasoning, usually salt and pepper, if you think it is necessary.

B

BAKE
To cook with hot, dry air in an oven.

BAKING POWDER
Made from **baking soda**, baking powder makes some doughs and batters rise during baking.

BAKING SODA
A white powder that, when combined with an acidic liquid such as buttermilk, produces carbon dioxide gas bubbles, which make batters rise during baking.

BASTE
To keep food moist during cooking by spooning or brushing on sauce, melted butter, or other liquid.

BATCH
The quantity of food cooked or baked at one time, such as a batch of cookies.

BATTER
An uncooked mixture that is thin enough to pour, such as cake or pancake batter, usually containing eggs, flour, and liquid.

BEAT
To mix ingredients vigorously, using a continuous circular motion. Beating incorporates air into mixtures.

BLEND
1. To combine two or more ingredients thoroughly.
2. To mix ingredients in an electric blender.

BOIL
1. To heat a liquid until bubbles constantly rise to the surface and break.
2. To cook food in a boiling liquid, whether it is a gentle boil, with small bubbles rising slowly and breaking mildly, or a rapid boil, with many large bubbles rising and breaking quickly. At sea level, water boils at 212 degrees Fahrenheit (212°F). The temperature will stay at 212°F whether the liquid is boiling gently or rapidly.

BROIL
To cook directly under a flame or a heating unit such as an electric broiler.

BROILER
An appliance that broils food, usually built into the top of an oven. The food is placed on a broiler tray and put on an oven shelf positioned under the broiler.

BROWN
To cook food until it turns a light golden or dark brown color.

BRUSH
To coat with a light layer of liquid, such as melted butter or milk, using a small brush.

BUTTER, UNSALTED
Stores sell both salted and unsalted butter. Many recipes call for unsalted butter because it lets the cook add salt to taste.

C

CHILL
To place food in the refrigerator until cold.

CHOCOLATE
Made from the seeds (or "beans") of the tropical cacao tree, chocolate is one of the world's favorite flavors. Cooks can buy chocolate in many different forms, including **semisweet chocolate,** which is a dark, sweet chocolate sold as bars and chips; and **unsweetened chocolate,** which tastes bitter but gives a very strong chocolate flavor to recipes. It is sold in small squares. **Unsweetened cocoa powder** (different than hot cocoa mix) is a fine powder of pure chocolate.

CHOP
To cut food into pieces. Finely chopped means small pieces; coarsely chopped means large pieces.

COAT
To cover the surface of a food or piece of equipment with butter, flour, crumbs, or other ingredients.

COMBINE
To mix together two or more ingredients, either dry or wet.

COOL (COMPLETELY)
To let something hot sit at room temperature until it is no longer warm to the touch, or until it has cooled completely to room temperature.

CORE

To remove the center part (the core and seeds) from fruits, such as apples and pears, and vegetables.

CREAM

The richest part of whole milk, cream is used to give extra richness to sauces and desserts. Depending on how much fat the cream contains, it will be given a more specific name. **Half-and-half** is a light mixture made of equal parts milk and cream. **Heavy cream** is at least 36 percent fat, and is sometimes sold as **whipping cream** because it is the cream to buy when you want to make a thick, whipped topping for desserts. Cream will whip best if you chill the beaters and bowl for about an hour first.

CROSSWISE

In the same direction as, or parallel to, a piece of food's shortest side.

D

DASH

A few drops of a liquid ingredient; less than ⅛ teaspoon.

DIAMETER

The widest measure across a round object, such as a pie plate or round of pastry dough.

DICE

To cut food into small cubes.

DOUGH

An uncooked mixture usually containing flour, liquid, and seasonings that is soft enough to be worked with your hands, but is too stiff to pour.

DRAIN

To pour off liquid.

DRIZZLE

To pour liquid or icing in a stream, zigzag style, over food.

DUST

To cover a food, your hands, or a work surface very lightly with a powdery substance such as flour. Confectioners' sugar is often dusted on desserts with a sifter or sieve.

E

EGGS

Sold in a range of sizes. Large eggs should be used for the recipes in this book. Eggs add moisture and richness to batters and doughs.

To separate an egg, over a small bowl, crack an egg. Gently pull the shell apart, trapping the unbroken yolk in the shell and letting the white fall into the bowl. Put the yolk in a separate bowl.

F

FAHRENHEIT (°F)

A temperature scale in which 32° (32 degrees) represents the point at which water freezes and 212° the point at which water boils. Oven temperature is indicated by °F.

FLOUR, ALL-PURPOSE

The most common kind of flour used in cooking and baking. All-purpose flour is available bleached and unbleached.

FOLD

To combine ingredients gently, usually with a rubber spatula, using a special circular motion. As the mixing bowl is gradually turned, the spatula cuts straight down through the center of the ingredients, under them, up along the side of the bowl, and back over to the center.

G

GARLIC CLOVE

One small segment taken from the larger whole bulb (or "head") of garlic.

GARNISH

1. To decorate a dish before serving.
2. The food used to decorate a dish before serving.

GRATE

To rub food, such as cheese, against a surface that has many small, sharp-edged rasps (like a kitchen grater) to make fine little particles.

GREASE

To rub a surface of a pan or dish with fat, such as butter or shortening, to keep food from sticking.

H

HEAT, STOVE

When food is cooked on top of a stove, a recipe should tell you how much heat to use. Heat levels are marked on the dial or buttons that control the burner. Low heat is usually just above the lowest setting, which recipes sometimes call very low; medium heat is when the dial is turned on about halfway; and high heat comes when the dial is at its highest setting. Medium-low and medium-high heats are midway between those pairs of settings. With a gas burner, you can actually see the flame to help you judge how high or low you set the heat.

K

KABOB
Bite-size pieces of food threaded onto a skewer.

KNEAD
To work dough with your hands using a pressing, folding, turning motion. When dough is fully kneaded, it becomes smooth and elastic.

L

LENGTHWISE
In the same direction as, or parallel to, a piece of food's longest side.

M

MARINADE
A flavored liquid in which ingredients are soaked to give them flavor or make them tender.

MARINATE
To soak an ingredient in a marinade.

MEASURE
To place an ingredient in a measuring cup or measuring spoon to ensure an exact amount. There are flat-topped measuring cups for dry ingredients and measuring cups with pouring spouts for wet ingredients. Small amounts of dry and wet ingredients are measured in the same style of measuring spoon.

MELT
To heat a solid substance, such as butter, until it becomes liquid.

P

PEEL
To remove the outside skin or covering (the peel) from fruits, such as oranges and pears, and vegetables, such as onions.

PINCH
The amount of a dry ingredient that you can pick up or "pinch" between your thumb and forefinger; less than ⅛ teaspoon.

PIPE
To apply icing as a decoration to a cake or cookie using a piping bag and decorating or writing tip.

PREHEAT
To heat the oven or broiler to a certain temperature before putting food in to cook. Preheat an oven for at least 15 minutes.

Q

QUARTER
To cut food, often through its center, into four equal parts.

R

REFRIGERATE
To place food in the refrigerator to chill and sometimes to become firmer in texture.

ROAST
To cook in an oven with hot dry heat, usually referring to meats rather than baked goods.

ROOM TEMPERATURE
The temperature of a comfortable room, not too hot or too cold. Butter is often brought to room temperature before it is combined with other ingredients, so it will soften slightly and blend more easily.

ROOT END
The end of a vegetable, such as an onion, from which its roots once grew, opposite the leaf end. Even though onions sold in the store have been trimmed, you can still see and feel the nubby texture of the roots at one end and the dry edges of the trimmed leaves at the other.

ROUNDED
Used to describe an overly full teaspoon or tablespoon measure.

S

SALT
A mineral that comes from both the land and the sea. Salt highlights the flavor of most ingredients, keeping foods from tasting bland.

SAUTÉ
To cook food quickly, over medium-high or high heat, with a small amount of fat or oil. Usually done in a shallow, straight or slope-sided pan.

SEASONING
Any ingredient added to food to give it more flavor, such as salt, pepper, other spices, herbs, and sometimes sugar or citrus juice.

SEED
To remove the seed or seeds from vegetables or fruit.

SET/UNTIL SET
When a liquid congeals as it cooks or cools, becoming firm.

SET ASIDE

To put food off to one side while you do something else.

SHORTENING

A kind of solid cooking fat made from vegetable oil and used in cooking and baking.

SIFT

To pass a dry ingredient such as flour or confectioners' sugar through a sieve or strainer, to make it finer. This allows it to blend more evenly with other ingredients or to evenly decorate a surface.

SIMMER

To cook a liquid, or ingredients in a liquid, just below the boiling point. Bubbles form during simmering but do not break through the surface of the liquid. The surface of simmering liquid looks like it is quivering.

SLICE

To cut across food with a knife, making pieces that are thick or thin.

SOFTEN

To let an ingredient such as butter sit at room temperature until soft enough to spread.

SPRINKLE

To scatter one or more ingredients over a surface.

STIR

To move a utensil such as a spoon, fork, or whisk continually through dry or wet ingredients, usually in a circular pattern. Sometimes you stir ingredients just until they are combined and sometimes until they are smooth.

SUGAR

Cooks use many different types of sugar to sweeten dishes. Three of the most common: **Granulated sugar** is the familiar white kind, which comes in small granules that pour easily. **Brown sugar** is a kind of granulated sugar that gets its rich flavor and brown color from the addition of molasses. It is available in light and dark varieties; the dark has a stronger flavor. Because it is sticky and clumpy, brown sugar should be firmly packed down in the cup for accurate measuring. **Confectioners' sugar** is white sugar that has been ground to a fine powder and mixed with a little cornstarch to prevent clumping. It is used to make icing and is also dusted on desserts for decoration.

T

TENDER

Describes food that is cooked until soft enough to bite and chew easily, but that is not mushy.

THAW

To let a frozen food sit in the refrigerator or at room temperature until it is no longer frozen. If you need to thaw an ingredient slowly and gently, put it in the refrigerator.

THICKEN

When a food changes from a looser, more liquid texture to a thicker, firmer texture.

THIN

To add liquid to a thick mixture to make it more liquid. Milk or cream can be added to icing to thin it and make it easier to spread.

TOSS

To mix ingredients lightly by tumbling them together with your hands, two forks, or two spoons.

TOUGH

Describes food that is difficult to chew, sometimes because it has been undercooked and sometimes because it has been cooked too long.

TRIM

To cut away from food any part that you don't need, to make something even in shape and size, or to cut away something that is not in good enough condition to eat.

V

VANILLA EXTRACT

A flavoring made from vanilla beans. Vanilla beans are the dried pods of a type of orchid.

W

WHIP

To beat ingredients rapidly so they become full of air and increase in volume.

WORK SURFACE

A flat space where you can cut up, mix, or prepare foods. It is important to keep your work surface clean and dry while cooking.

Z

ZEST

The thin, brightly colored outer layer of the peel of a citrus fruit such as an orange. It is sometimes grated or cut off in very thin strips to add flavor to recipes.

INDEX

acorn squash, baked, with maple cream 72
apples
    caramel 69
    coring 13
    cranberry sauce with orange and 74
    haroset 28
asparagus
    preparing 9
    springtime 35

be mine cookies 22
beverages
    carolers' hot chocolate 103
    spiced cider 65
    summertime confetti punch 11
biscuits, buttermilk 39
blueberry bowl, red, white, and 54
bread
    buttermilk biscuits 39
    Christmas morning French toast 87
    corn kernel spoon 94
    great turkey melt 78
    hero sandwiches 53
    New Year's toasts 104
    popovers 96
    pumpkin 71
    raisin scones 47
brownies, chocolate chip Passover 31
buttermilk biscuits 39

caramel apples 69
cheese
    great turkey melt 78
    patriotic nachos 59
chicken
    best roast 80
    and vegetable kabobs 56
chocolate
    carolers' hot 103
    chocolate chip Passover brownies 31
    devil's food cupcakes 66
    fondue 107
Christmas 14–15
    carolers' hot chocolate 103
    corn kernel spoon bread 94
    crisp vegetable wreath with herb-yogurt dip 88
    festive winter salad 93
    holiday cookies 100
    mashed sweet potatoes with brown sugar and pecans 91
    morning French toast 87
    old-fashioned gingerbread 99
    popovers 96
cider, spiced 65
coconut meringue nests 36
cookies
    basic butter cookie dough 17
    be mine 22
    chocolate chip Passover brownies 31
    coconut meringue nests 36
    Halloween spice 63
    holiday 100
    rolling and cutting 17
corn
    on the cob, butter-roasted 61
    kernel spoon bread 94

cranberry sauce with apple and orange 74
cupcakes, devil's food 66

Easter 8–9
    buttermilk biscuits 39
    coconut meringue nests 36
    eggs, naturally perfect 32
    springtime asparagus 35
    strawberry tartlets 41
eggs
    coconut meringue nests 36
    naturally perfect Easter 32
    soft-cooked 42

Father's Day 10
    favorite potato salad 50
    frozen fruit pops 49
    hero sandwiches 53
fondue, chocolate 107
Fourth of July 11
    butter-roasted corn on the cob 61
    chicken and vegetable kabobs 56
    patriotic nachos 59
    red, white, and blueberry bowl 54
French toast, Christmas morning 87
fruit. See also individual fruits
    bowl, melon and berry 45
    chocolate fondue 107
    pops, frozen 49
    red, white, and blueberry bowl 54

gelt, golden 84
gingerbread, old-fashioned 99

Halloween 12
    caramel apples 69
    devil's food cupcakes 66
    spice cookies 63
    spiced cider 65
Hanukkah 14
    best roast chicken 80
    golden gelt 84
    holiday cookies 100
    potato latkes 83
haroset 28
heart-shaped waffles 21
hero sandwiches 53
holiday cookies 100

icing, basic 18
Independence Day. See Fourth of July

kabobs, chicken and vegetable 56

latkes, potato 83

matzo ball soup 27
melon and berry fruit bowl 45
mints, valentine 25
Mother's Day 9
    melon and berry fruit bowl 45
    raisin scones 47
    soft-cooked eggs 42

nachos, patriotic 59
New Year's 15
    chocolate fondue 107
    toasts 104

oranges
    cranberry sauce with apple and 74
    golden gelt 84

Passover 9
    brownies, chocolate chip 31
    haroset 28
    matzo ball soup 27
pears, peeling 15
pies
    basic pie pastry 16
    favorite pumpkin 77
popovers 96
pops, frozen fruit 49
potatoes
    latkes 83
    salad, favorite 50
pumpkin
    bread 71
    pie, favorite 77
punch, summertime confetti 11

raisin scones 47
red, white, and blueberry bowl 54

safety tips 19
salads
    favorite potato 50
    festive winter 93
sandwiches
    great turkey melt 78
    hero 53
scones, raisin 47
soup, matzo ball 27
spoon bread, corn kernel 94
springtime asparagus 35
squash, baked acorn, with maple cream 72
strawberries
    frozen fruit pops 49
    melon and berry fruit bowl 45
    preparing 9
    red, white, and blueberry bowl 54
    tartlets 41
summertime confetti punch 11
sweet potatoes, mashed, with brown sugar and pecans 91

tartlets, strawberry 41
Thanksgiving 13
    baked acorn squash with maple cream 72
    cranberry sauce with apple and orange 74
    favorite pumpkin pie 77
    great turkey melt 78
    pumpkin bread 71
toasts, New Year's 104
turkey melt, great 78

Valentine's Day 8
    be mine cookies 22
    heart-shaped waffles 21
    mints 25
vegetables. See also individual vegetables
    and chicken kabobs 56
    wreath, crisp, with herb-yogurt dip 88

waffles, heart-shaped 21
whipped cream, sweetened 18
wreath, crisp vegetable, with herb-yogurt dip 88

ACKNOWLEDGMENTS

The publishers would like to thank the following people and associations for their generous assistance and support in producing this book: Desne Border, Ken DellaPenta, Kathryn Meehan, Anna Preslar, Vivian Ross, and Hill Nutrition Associates.

The following kindly lent props for photography: Mazeltov Gifts and Ma Maison, San Francisco, CA. The photographer would like to thank Tammy and Mark Becker for generously sharing their home for location photography. She would also like to thank ProCamera, San Francisco, CA, and FUJI film for their generous support of this project. Special acknowledgment goes to Erin Quon and Kim Brent.